THE SOUTH

THE SOUTH

A Central Theme?

Edited by MONROE L. BILLINGTON
New Mexico State University

HOLT, RINEHART AND WINSTON
New York · Chicago · San Francisco · Atlanta
Dallas · Montreal · Toronto · London · Sydney

Cover illustration: Rienzi Plantation, Thibodaux, Louisiana.
Presently owned by Lawrence Levert. (*Photograph by
Clifford L. Snyder*)

CONTENTS

"The Queen of Industry, or The New South." Cartoon by Thomas Nast. (From *Harper's Weekly,* January 14, 1882)

Introduction

The South has been identified as a distinct region of the United States since the early days of the Republic. Charles Pinckney's declaration in 1787, "When I say Southern, I mean Maryland, and the states to the southward of her," was concerned with geographical boundaries, but its implications for the future were clear. Pinckney anticipated what the next generation of Americans on both sides of the Mason-Dixon line came to believe: that the South as a section possessed a separate and unique identity. The South was not the only area of the nation that developed specific sectional characteristics, but throughout the course of American history contemporary writers and historians have generally recognized it as the region most different from the remainder of the country. Visitors to the South during the first half of the nineteenth century saw the region as distinct, and they both influenced and were influenced by those who stressed the South's uniqueness. Alexis de Tocqueville, Frederick Law Olmsted, Frances Kemble, and others wrote many pages describing or reflecting upon this region which appeared to be out of the mainstream of the American experience.

When the South developed its distinctive characteristics and, more important, how a consciousness of the region's separateness evolved are questions still being debated. John R. Alden[1] writes that the South's awareness of itself first appeared with the discovery of nationalism during the American Revolution, although most historians elaborating the identity theme date the development of the region's self-consciousness from the sectional controversies of the 1820s and subsequent years. John G. Van Deusen[2] finds that Southern sectionalism emerged from the depression following the Panic of 1819; Glover Moore[3] sees sectional animosities growing out of the 1820 debates on slavery and territorial expansion; and Joseph C. Robert[4] states that the peculiarly Southern attitudes resulted from Nat Turner's revolt and its implications. Regardless of when the political, economic, societal, and attitudinal differences between the South and the remainder of the nation began, they were clearly evident by 1861 and they combined to play a part in bringing on a bloody conflict.

Although the Civil War held the Union together, the impact of the war and the Reconstruction era sustained sectional feeling, particularly in the former Confederate states. Northern attempts to reconcile the South with the Union were unsuccessful,

---

[1] *The First South* (Baton Rouge, 1961).

[2] *Economic Basis of Disunion in South Carolina* (New York, 1928).

[3] *The Missouri Controversy, 1819–1821* (Lexington, Ky., 1953).

[4] *The Road from Monticello: A Study of the Virginia Slavery Debate of 1832* (Durham, 1941).

leading to a sharp Southern reaction against the victorious North. The development of the myth of an idealized ante-bellum civilization, the glorification of the war, economic doldrums, and the determination to maintain white supremacy by saddling the freed Negro with second-class status kept alive in the late nineteenth and early twentieth centuries the belief that Dixie was a land unto itself.

This is not to say that the South was of one mind or that its beliefs about itself and the rest of the nation were without dissenting voices. Diversity of geography led Frederick Jackson Turner to conclude that not *one* South but *many* Souths existed; he might have made the same comment with regard to southerners, who throughout the region's history have by no means expressed unanimity. In the ante-bellum period southerners differed sharply on such major issues as banking, tariff, land, and internal improvement policies, and John C. Calhoun had his detractors as well as his followers. Loyalism to the Union was not uncommon in the South during the Civil War, and after the military conflict Southern leaders who cooperated with the North in the economic realm, happy to be invited to "the great barbecue," were at the same time encouraging animus between the sections.

The technological revolution of the twentieth century played a large role in removing the legacies of the past and nudging the South into the mainstream of American life. With the advent of nationwide radio and television and the mass circulation of motion picture films, intellectual and cultural distinctions were diminished. Southerners and northerners came face to face via the automobile and the highway, and the result was direct communication, and in some cases understanding, for the first time. Along with the entire nation, the South was profoundly affected by the processes of urbanization, industrialization, and social change. Some writers conclude that by the 1960s the South was so much like the rest of the nation that the era of the South as a distinct section had come to an end. Others recognize the South as a separate section—whether remaining static or moving away from or toward the national ideal—and have spent hours attempting to identify those qualities or characteristics that set it apart. They have asked and attempted to answer questions such as: What is the South? Who is a southerner? What are the essential qualities of Southernism? Who speaks for the South? What makes the South a distinct region?

One of the approaches to the South has been the search for a central theme running through the South's past and revealing the inner nature of the region. In an essay entitled "The Central Theme of Southern History," Ulrich B. Phillips[5] advanced the thesis that Southern whites have resolved that above all else the South must remain a white man's country. Contending that this overriding conviction is the central theme of Southern history, Phillips held that southerners developed the doctrine of white supremacy as soon as Negroes became numerous enough to create a problem of race control. Writing in 1928 Phillips implied that the concept of the South would refer to a geographical region of the United States only if white supremacy were somehow overcome, but he assumed that white supremacy would remain forever with southerners. The use of the phrase

---

[5] *American Historical Review*, XXXIV (1928), 30–43.

"central theme" sent others in pursuit of answers that might solve the Southern mystery. After investigation, observation, and contemplation, many writers concluded that Phillips was correct: that the presence of the Negro gave the South distinctiveness. Other historians argued that the presence of an aristocracy was more crucial to the region's identity, while another group saw the influence of a bellicose attitude on the part of southerners as a prime determinant in the region's character. Still others turned to the South's agrarianism and the ideals of an agrarian society for the inner nature of the region, and a final group of writers explained the South in terms of regional, cultural, and intellectual traditions.

The first selection in this collection of readings is an updating by Francis B. Simkins of Phillips' contention that white racism constitutes the one facet of the South which makes the region different from the remainder of the nation. Recognizing that racism is not peculiar to southerners, Simkins holds that the particular set of events which occurred during and following Reconstruction gave Southern racism a special quality not found elsewhere. Like Phillips, Simkins believes that an end to the doctrine of white supremacy would destroy the reality of Southernism, but he cannot conceive of a time when white supremacy will not exist in the South.

The authors of the next three selections, agreeing that the Negro has been vital in the South's development, have proceeded to elaborate or modify the Phillips statement. George B. Tindall addressed himself to the central-theme thesis some thirty years after Phillips first advanced it, and he concludes that a preoccupation with race—including its mythology and symbolism—has been the keystone in the structure of Southern society in the twentieth century. Noting the crumbling of the ideological defense of white supremacy in the 1950s, Tindall states that in view of changing conditions the issue of race can no longer be considered a necessary feature of Southern life. He indicates that an identifiable South will remain for years to come; however, disagreeing with Phillips, he states that the region's future is related to much more than a system of segregation and proscription.

Thomas D. Clark states that the Negro and his relationship with the white southerner have constituted the distinguishing features of the Southern way of life. He documents the rapid erosion of old patterns of race relations at mid-century, as well as the southerner's resistance to the recent advances of the Negro. Implicit in his discussion is a changing—if not a vanishing—South.

In the final selection dealing with the presence of the Negro, Harry S. Ashmore describes the essentials of modern Southernism as the institutions of share tenancy, one-partyism, and segregation of the races, which developed with the abolition of slavery after the Civil War. He points out that share tenancy provided an outlet for the former slave's labor; one-party politics controlled the Negro's political power; and Jim Crow practices circumscribed the social contact of the two races. In recent years these institutions have been profoundly altered: sharecropping declined after 1930; a viable two-party system was in its infancy in the South by 1950; and events after World War II indicated the forming of irreparable cracks in the color wall. These internal changes were aided by powerful external forces that coalesced to diminish the South's separate status. In contrast to the views of Simkins and Tindall, Ashmore predicts the imminent death of the South and has written an "epitaph for Dixie." Are traditional Southern racial attitudes weakening as a result of overpowering economic and social change? If so, will the South disappear as a distinct region when southerners cease to be preoccupied with the race question?

While some authorities have explained the South in terms of the presence of slavery and the Negro, others have stated that the men at the apex of the social structure have been the chief determinant in the region's distinctiveness. They have stressed the importance of the landed gentry and the attitudes all classes of southerners developed toward that ruling clique. In his book, *The First Gentlemen of Virginia*, Louis B. Wright contends that the colonial society of early Virginia was dominated by a "tight little aristocracy" which patterned its ways after the English ruling class. Wright concludes that a native aristocracy quickly grew up in colonial Virginia, and the presence of this politically and economically powerful landed gentry affected all of Southern colonial society. Writing with a broader viewpoint, another historian[6] has suggested that the prevalence of the country gentleman ideal—a pattern of society borrowed from the English, justified by French physiocrats, and taking root naturally in the agricultural South—best explains the entire region. In the next selection, Clement Eaton agrees and notes that the ideal of the country gentleman was carried by emigrating Virginians and Carolinians to all corners of the South.

Focusing primarily on the ante-bellum South, Rollin G. Osterweis believes that the civilization of the Old South was supported by a tripod made up of a cotton-plantation system, Negro slavery, and a cult of chivalry adhered to by Southern aristocrats. Directing his discussion toward the latter—the neglected leg of the tripod—Osterweis argues that the impact of the ideals of chivalry on southerners continues to be felt today, while the influence of the plantation system and the institution of slavery is no longer present. The South's concern for honor, manners, and hospitality today stems from the attention Old South aristocrats gave to a chivalric cult. Thus, chivalry has been a more constant theme in Southern history than the other two major factors. Recent writers have pointed out that leisure and the concept of personal freedom also influenced the southerner's mind, habit, and society.[7] Intense individualism, defense of local rights, and paternalism toward "my people" were additional elements in this aristocratic tradition.

Acknowledging the presence of an aristocracy in the years prior to the Civil War, Francis B. Simkins argues that white southerners learned from their defeat in the war the lack of wisdom in stressing their aristocratic past. He sees southerners after the war assuming a pose in order to create the myth that the South was democratic like the rest of the nation. He writes that twentieth-century southerners honestly believe in a caste system, that they can control the Negro with it and thereby protect their own liberty—which southerners hold in higher regard than equality. The presence of demagogues and lynch mobs during the South's democratic periods and the existence of a comparatively

---

[6] Avery Craven, *The Repressible Conflict, 1830–1861* (University, La., 1939).

[7] David Bertelson, *The Lazy South* (New York, 1967).

open society during Thomas Jefferson's time indicate that the most democratic eras of Southern society were the most conservative and that the most aristocratic periods were the most liberal.

In a selection from *The Militant South,* John Hope Franklin writes that ante-bellum Southern society was afflicted with a martial spirit brought about by the glorification of war, by southerners' long careers as frontiersmen and Indian fighters, by the region's deficient political system, and by the organization and discipline Southern whites effected to maintain the institution of slavery. Violence was inextricably woven into the fabric of Southern society, and it constituted an important element in the total experience of southerners. Implicit in Franklin's volume is the bellicosity of southerners as the region's central theme.

Franklin writes about militancy in the South before 1861, but Frank E. Vandiver extends the concept of the southerner as extremist into the modern age. He suggests that the most constant theme in the Southern experience has been "response to challenge." Building upon Franklin's base, Vandiver attempts to explain the southerner's extremism in the nineteenth and twentieth centuries not only in terms of his past environment but also in terms of forces outside the South. Southerners' extreme reactions have been triggered by "aggravated provocation," and Northern, federal, and Negro pressures have set off the "offensive-defensive mechanism" of militant southerners, bringing bloodshed and death in the twentieth century as well as in the nineteenth.

Since the first white men settled on the shores of Virginia in 1607, the South has been predominantly a rural area. For over 350 years the southerner has followed the biblical injunction to till the soil by the sweat of the brow, growing both food for his table and staple crops for the use of others. Charles W. Ramsdell has indicated that the region's overriding attention to agriculture, particularly cotton, tobacco, and sugar, constitutes the most constant factor—and thus the central theme—in the South's history. This preoccupation with the cultivation of the soil has given the South's agricultural classes a crucial role in determining the conditions of Southern life and the patterns of its thinking. Ramsdell admits that poverty, the race problem, the consciousness of the South as a sectional minority, and the development of industry were additional components in the regional equation. While he holds that none of these factors was as significant a determinant as agriculture, he recognizes that as industry developed in the South, the region's devotion to agriculture began to weaken.

When twelve southerners in 1930 saw the South gradually bartering away its tranquil agricultural ways for the gaudy benefits of industrialization, they raised their voices against the trend, elaborating their objections in a book of essays entitled *I'll Take My Stand.* These agrarians did not want the South to surrender its unique agricultural tradition and culture for dubious material gain. They sought to defend the Southern way of life against the American way, and they agreed that the phrase "Agrarian *versus* Industrial" best represented that distinction. The following selection is composed of two excerpts from this "agrarian manifesto." Frank L. Owsley directs his attention to the coming of the Civil War, which he says resulted from the fundamental differences existing between two sections, one commercial and industrial and the other agrarian. Although his essay is concerned primarily with the "irrepressible conflict," he equates the South with agrarianism, stating that the South was distinct because it was the seat of an agrarian civilization in a nation bent on industrialization. John Crowe Ransom carries the concept of the agrarian South into the period after the Civil War. While he majors on the malignancy of industrialism, he makes it clear that the values and ways of the agrarian South set it apart from the North. He issues a call to all southerners to resist growing industrialism in their region in order to maintain a traditional agrarian philosophy.

Thirty years after the agrarian manifesto was published, David M. Potter saw the nation being overpowered by a pervasive urban-industrial culture. He found the South's past and future bound up in the survival of a meaningful folk culture rather than in its agricultural traditions. Potter does not argue that this folk culture, which survived into the age of the bulldozer, is ideal or utopian, although he does state that it has a relatedness and meaning not found in the materialistic mass culture. He is convinced that it is the key to an understanding of the South.

C. Vann Woodward suggests that the South's distinctiveness lies in its history, that is, in "the collective experience" of the Southern people. He points out that Americans generally have known abundance, while southerners have known poverty; that the United States has experienced success, whereas the South has known frustration, failure, and defeat, including not only military defeat in the Civil War but also the frustration of Reconstruction and long decades of failure in economic, social, and political life; that Americans have known innocence, even as the South has felt guilt; that Americans were "born free," yet southerners were not, since they had and have the problems of the slave and the Negro. Thus, Woodward argues that the South has had a tragic history and that this has helped unify the section and contribute to its uniqueness.

Perhaps the writers who have searched for the essence of Southernism in the region's agrarian folk culture or in its unique past are in reality grappling with one aspect of a larger topic: the South's conservatism. Concerned with the South of the twentieth century, James Jackson Kilpatrick sees a basically conservative regional civilization and culture based upon a reverence for tradition and good manners, the desire for liberty (not to say equality), and the attempt to resist industrialism by upholding old agrarian ideals and ways. Above all, he relates the South's conservatism to states' rights, and he uses that concept as a justification for many of the South's actions in recent years, especially regarding race relations. He contends that the Southern states collectively represent the final hope for the continued existence of a conservative philosophy in the United States.

The grouping of the selections in this volume under five separate headings should not leave the reader with the impression that the writers have stressed one theme to the exclusion of all others. Indeed, almost every selection deals with more than one theme, as the authors write about what has made the South distinctive. Slavery would not have developed or remained in the South had not the region lent itself to a plantation economy. The presence of slavery presupposes the presence of a ruling class. The gentlemen of the South in turn had an affinity for the soil, and agrarian values loomed large in the South.

The mind of the South—whether its bellicosity, its political inclinations, its yearning for a folk culture, or its grasping of the past—has surely been much influenced by the presence of the Negro, the aristocratic tradition, and the agrarian way of life. Without these, the South would not have possessed such a high degree of cultural unity. Each has contributed to the total picture of what the South has been in the past and what it remains today.

Considering the schools of thought represented in this volume, what may be said about the South's separateness? What will become of the South as a concept as more and more Negroes migrate from the region and as Southern attitudes on race change? Has the growth of a larger and more economically solvent middle class in the South undercut the strength of the aristocratic tradition? Does a quality of belligerency explain Southern reactions in the years prior to 1861 and in the post-World War II upheaval of Southern society? Have provincialism and tradition been crucial as the South's distinguishing attributes? Can a consciousness of history instill new myths in the minds of the region's inhabitants, unduly prolonging the belief that the South remains unique?

The quest for a central theme revealing the inner nature of the region has been responsible for the development of valuable insights useful to an understanding of the South. Since the concept of the South has had a powerful impact upon the nation's history, consideration of this question should lead to a better understanding not only of the South as an identifiable region but of the nation as a whole.

In the reprinted selections footnotes appearing in the original sources have in general been omitted unless they contribute to the argument or better understanding of the selection.

FRANCIS B. SIMKINS (1898–1966), born in South
Carolina and for thirty-eight years professor of history at
Longwood College in Farmville, Virginia, was one of the
most provocative writers of Southern history. Besides
numerous interpretative essays, Simkins wrote a history of
Reconstruction in South Carolina, a biography of Benjamin
Tillman, and a popular college text on the South.
Throughout his writings, Simkins resolutely held that a
distinctive South exists, that it has a mind and culture of its
own, and that it not only is different from the remainder of
the nation but has every right to be. In the brief essay below
he reiterates Ulrich B. Phillips' famous contention that white
supremacy is the one characteristic above all which lends
distinctiveness to the region below the Potomac. In view of
the significant changes that have occurred on the Southern
scene in the past decade, it should be noted that Simkins'
point of view is now historical rather than current.*

Francis B. Simkins

Unchanging White Supremacy

Abraham Lincoln was right in saying that
the South could not exist as an independent
nation. The region below the Potomac did not
wish to break what Lincoln called "the mystic
cords of memory" with the rest of the United
States. It was and is more like the region
above the Potomac than like any other part of
the world. It had the same religion, the same
ideals, the same notions of democracy and the
same race prejudices. In the crisis of the Civil
War, an important minority in every
Southern state except South Carolina opposed secession.

Many Southerners fought on the Union
side. The Unionist plan of invasion was de-
vised by Winfield Scott, a Virginian. The

Unionist counterpart of Stonewall Jackson
was the Rock of Chickamauga, George H.
Thomas, another Virginian. The surrender
at Appomattox did not mark the death of a
nation; it was the death of an entity without a
national soul, the submission of something
that would never, like Ireland or Poland, rise
as an immortal nation. The most rabid
Yankee-hater today wants to be a patriotic
American.

When Southern hatred of the North was at
its height, because of the presence of carpetbaggers, Southerners breathed patriotic ven-
geance against Spain because that country
put to death Americans caught filibustering.
The South went into a patriotic delirium

*Francis B. Simkins, "Unchanging White Supremacy." *Current History,* XXXV (November 1958), 282–286.
Portions of this essay originally appeared in Simkins' introduction to Ina D. Van Noppen, *The South, A Docu-
mentary History* (Princeton, N.J.: D. Van Nostrand Company, Inc., 1958). Reprinted by permission of Current
History and D. Van Nostrand Company, Inc.

when the chance came to fight Spain for the American nation in 1898; this was true also in 1917 and in 1941.

The stalwart Americanism of Southerners has led optimists many times to predict the imminent extinction of the South as an entity distinct from the rest of the United States. As early as 1879, Frederick Douglass, a famous Negro leader, declared that conditions in the Southern states were so steadily improving "that the colored man will ultimately realize the fullest measure of liberty and equality accorded and secured in any section of our common country." James W. Garner, a competent Southern historian, asserted in 1914 that the time had come for the section to "emancipate herself from the deadly one-party system" because the Negro question had been settled for the indefinite future.

The legend reached an ultimate extreme in a book written in 1926 by a distinguished Vanderbilt University professor [Edwin Mims] entitled *The Advancing South,* containing a chapter called "The Ebbing Tide of Color." This was followed in 1948 by the assertion of Harry S. Ashmore, the Arkansas editor, that the increased voting of the Negro in the democratic primaries makes the race a "patent, positive factor in the region" and "the passing of the one-party system inevitable." Mr. Ashmore followed up these assertions ten years later with a book called *A Requiem for Dixie.*[1] Robert Penn Warren, who built a resounding reputation as a novelist and essayist on emphasis on Southern distinctiveness, proclaims in 1958 in an anthology of Southern short stories that "perhaps twenty years from now there will be no place for a collection of Southern writers" because regional differences are being destroyed.

There are grounds for predictions that the identity of the South is being absorbed into

the national unity. The region drove away with shotguns the first generation of carpetbaggers, but it welcomed second and third generations of "carpetbaggers" armed with capital to invest. Much of the Southern landscape has been bulldozed out of its original shape to make clearings for Northern-owned industries. The South reads only books and magazines that have hit the New York sounding board. It has produced brilliant novelists who affront the ancestral pride by exposing the regional weaknesses. It has in imitation of the Middle West adopted "triumphant 'progressive' education which progresses even faster than the North and which has been rushing school systems off into a life of sin as fast as they are born." School houses, Northern style, have been "snowed" all over the South; the region spends a larger proportion of its income on education than any other section of the country. The Ohio idea of good roads has been so successfully applied that the Yankee tourist is able to hurl himself through Virginia by means of mile-long bridges and underwater tunnels, without having a chance to see the antiquities.

The reality of the vanishing South has been accepted so thoroughly by the spokesmen of the New South that a Harvard scholar [Paul H. Buck] uses their words as the basis for a book called *The Road to Reunion.* This author solemnly marks the end of the South as a protesting minority in 1898, the year of its fervent participation in the military crusade against Spain.

The facts of history do not justify the claim that the history of North-South relations has been a record of steady decline in the intersectional asperities. An examination of the evidence reveals a series of ups and downs in an everlasting battle between the forces making for sectional reconciliation and for sectional estrangement. The let-us-have peace sentiments at Appomattox were followed by the

---

[1]This volume was published under the title: *An Epitaph for Dixie* (New York: W. W. Norton & Company, Inc., 1957). An excerpt from it appears in this book of readings.—Ed.

hates of Reconstruction. The good will created by the surrender in 1877 of the North on the Reconstruction issue was followed by the ill will created by the Lodge Force Bill of 1890 and by the disfranchising amendments to the Southern state constitutions. The amity created by the pronouncements of Booker T. Washington was dimmed by the affronts to caste caused by the ravings of the muckrakers and Theodore Roosevelt's appointment of Negroes to office.

The sense of national pride engendered in Southern hearts by the election of Woodrow Wilson and the victories of the First World War was followed by attacks upon the South "more abusive and unrelenting than anything the Southern states have experienced since the last Federal soldier was withdrawn from their soil." There were the Ku Klux exposures, ridicule of Southern political and religious attitudes, and the uncovering of alleged abuses of justice. The good will created between Franklin D. Roosevelt and the South was followed by legislation which affronted the traditions of the region. The willingness of the South to bear its share of the armed crusade to impose American ideals of equality upon Japan and Germany was followed by the demand that the South apply these ideals to the Negro. An atmosphere of resentment bitterer than ever before was created by the decree of the Supreme Court in 1954 that the two races be mixed in school.

The South has changed, but novelist Stark Young sapiently says, "The changing South is still the South." There is an education that does not educate. Northern bias in textbooks is offset by the effective indoctrination of local concepts that survive the regimentation of the schools. The home, not the school, determines the cultural outlook of the Southern child. The public is unused to listening to the collective opinions of school officials. Even lessons in a subject as "scientific" as cooking do not change fundamentally the character of the home diet.

There is danger of overemphasizing literary materials in measuring the outlook of a people as non-literary as those of the south. Most Southerners ignore the realistic writings pointing out the evil aspects of life in their section. They are nourished on the self-flattery of sentimental romances. The stark portrayals of William Faulkner and Ellen Glasgow do not reach to the level of the women's clubs. The more literate get only vicarious experience out of the critical appraisals of the region. They get the sentimental pleasure of enjoying between the covers of a book what they have no idea of sharing in actual life.

Legend to the contrary, the South has never objected to new machines. The reason is that Southerners do not fear that such physical changes will bring about changes in inherited ways. The most conservative of all inhabitants of the region are the Poor Whites. They have flocked into the cotton mills, where, in exchange for the one-mule plow of their primitive farms, they have established intimate relations with the most modern machinery New England affords. Yet intellectually and psychologically the Poor Whites awaken to the newness of their environment only to the extent of recovering some of the religious orthodoxies their forebears brought from England.

Cities and revolutions go hand in hand, say the historians of civilization. So it is assumed that the sensational growth of Southern cities has led to changes in the regional attitudes. Except in a physical sense the South has no cities in the Northern or European sense. Here is the case of "country-cracker-come-to-town." The country has conquered the city instead of the other way around. The urbanites vote the same way as their country cousins and go to church more often. If they can afford luxuries, they live within the city in rural-styled mansions with flowers and spacious gardens. They are more interested in hogs, horses, dogs and cows than in such urban diversions as music, painting, books and theaters. They dream of the time when success in business will make possible retirement to country estates.

Kindly Northern businessmen have been in the forefront of those who advocate that the South give up its peculiar ways in order to get the fullest benefits from the American way of life. They have given funds for Negro uplift and even for assaults on the color line. But these Northerners are careful not to interfere with the chances of success of their earth-shaking business investments by interfering with Southern customs. They employ native Southern whites to work in their shops and factories instead of "carpetbaggers." Only in a few cases do they give jobs to Negroes. Northern migrants to the South have learned a lesson from history: success may be obtained by leaving the "carpetbaggers" behind and denying employment opportunities to Negroes.

Ulrich B. Phillips, an authoritative delineator of the Southern way of life, says that "the central theme" of Southern history is white supremacy. This is the belief that there can be no cordiality between the races except when the Negro is willing to assume a position of social inferiority. This theme is what makes the South different from the rest of the world. Nowhere else in the annals of civilization have two fecund and numerous races dwelt together in the same communities without mixing. For a white woman to have an offspring by a Negro man has from the early days of colonization been anathema. The offspring of a Negro woman by a white man must take the social status of the Negro. . . .

The period of Southern history in which there was no military invasion or other act of violence is regarded by both liberal and conservative Southerners as the region's most horrible experience. This was Reconstruction, the time immediately after the Civil War when the radicals of the North tried to abolish aspects of the Southern color line. Of this period the *Encyclopedia Britannica* in a recent edition solemnly declared: "All the misfortunes of war itself are insignificant when compared with the suffering of the people during the era of Reconstruction." It was the time when the whites "had gone crazy with anger or were obsessed with some fearful mania" because "gibbering, louse-eaten, devil-worshipping barbarians from the jungles of Dahomey" were in legislative halls.

These opinions were not erratic because they were bound up with the very soul of the regional identity. To kill a Southerner in battle would be followed by his son rising up to defend the Southern cause more fervently than ever before. But to kill the doctrine of white supremacy would destroy the essence of Southernism, reduce the region to a mere geographical segment of the United States. Mongrelization would then perhaps create another Brazil or Cuba. The race mixtures of those two countries may be satisfactory to Brazilians and Cubans; but it would make the South into a parish province in the eyes of the rest of the United States. The prejudice in favor of racial separation is almost as deeply engrained in the region above the Potomac as in the region below that river.

Those who favor the abolition of regional differentials realistically emphasize the degree to which the South has desegregated in schools and other centers of community activity; for, as both the friends and enemies of the *status quo* in the South agree, the section would through race mixing lose those characteristics against which its critics complain.

The enemies of segregation have cause to be hopeful. The Federal courts and the

Justice Department of the United States have made dents in the sectional armor. The army makes white and colored boys drill together and sleep together in the same barracks. Many Southern church conventions have pronounced against segregation, and some Southern universities admit a few Negroes to their halls.

This attempt by official pressure to destroy the color line has made it tighter. No longer exist what an ante-bellum traveler called "the close cohabitation and association of black and white"; no longer do white men in appreciable numbers indulge in miscegenation; no longer, as in ante-bellum days, do the two races go to the same church. In the newer sections of the cities residential segregation is so complete that it is possible for a white person to pass years without contact with a single Negro.

Edwin R. Embree, a distinguished representative of the movement for inter-racial accord, admitted in 1933 the impossibility of "spontaneous and informal associations" between even the most well-disposed and enlightened members of both races. What was true then is true in 1958. The only "spontaneous and informal associations" between the two races that I have observed in those sections of the South where Negroes are numerous are among blacks and whites who on Saturdays lose their inhibitions in getting drunk together in the back of country stores.

The only Southerners that I know who advocate racial equality are a few college professors and ministers. They are able to do this because, ironically enough, they are the two elements of the white population who are most rigidly separated from the blacks by nature of their occupations. It is hard to say how these learned men would act if, like policemen and doctors, they were thrown into physical contact with Negroes. Not one of them has ever gone out of his way to meet a Negro in fraternal accord. It is not fair to

expect them to do this. It would mean social and occupational suicide.

There is a university in the South where much eloquence is spent in history and sociology classes advocating racial equality. A new professor could not get a position in that institution if he denied the innate equality of the races. But it never occurs to anyone on the campus to implement these sentiments. Distinctions of caste are accepted as unconsciously as rain or sunshine. . . .

The emptiness of Southern gestures in favor of interracial fraternity is illustrated by the behavior of a young man who had imbibed the latest teachings of psychology, sociology and anthropology on race in one of the South's most progressive colleges. How small an impression these teachings had made on his behavior was evident when he and I paid a visit to the rural community from which he had come. He went back to his natural Southern self by manifesting three tones in his voice: a normal tone for whites; a "mammy voice" for Negroes with whom he was familiar; and a haughty tone for strange Negroes. . . .

There have been revolutions in Southern agriculture and industry. Gigantic cities have developed. Poverty has largely vanished. There have been changes in politics and great improvements in the material well-being of the Negro. But these changes have not emotionally altered the region to any greater degree than the United States as a whole has been altered by the unparalleled physical and technological changes that have overtaken the nation in the last 150 years.

The United States adheres today as firmly as ever to the teachings of the Founding Fathers; the South holds on today as firmly as ever to its peculiar ideals and practices. Sherman and his 60 thousand invaders did not make a positive dint on Southern thinking processes 95 years ago; that cannot be done today except by methods more ruthless than those Sherman was willing to use.

In this article I have tried to demonstrate that national patriotism is not in conflict with regional loyalties and that the acceptance of imported ideas in literature, education and industry has not altered sectional attitudes. The South is obdurate in the matter of greatest importance, that of race. If I had the space I could demonstrate how the section has held its own in such important matters as religion, social customs and diet.

Despite assaults from without, the South is as proud as ever of its provincial ways. True Southerners are still warmed by what an adopted Southerner describes as their land "of varied forests and varied contour, from mountains to sea, a land of exceptional natural beauty" inhabited by a people who "impress one at once with their different voices, different accent, their sense of manners, the courtesy that appears in all classes, their organic folksiness (as if of one family), their awareness of the past as a force both hampering and helping."

A specialist in the history of the South since Reconstruction, GEORGE B. TINDALL (b. 1921) is author of *South Carolina Negroes, 1877–1900* (1952) and editor of *The Pursuit of Southern History* (1964) and *A Populist Reader* (1966). His *The Emergence of the New South, 1913–1945* (1967) provides a new understanding of the changing political and social climate in the twentieth-century South.

Tindall rejects Phillips' and Simkins' contention that white supremacy is the monistic central theme of Southern history, but at the same time he concludes that preoccupation with the mythology and symbolism of race has been of major concern in Southern thought. Tindall is a professor of history at the University of North Carolina at Chapel Hill.*

George B. Tindall

Mythology and Symbolism of Race

It is now more than thirty years since Ulrich Bonnell Phillips defined the unifying principle of southern history as "a common resolve indomitably maintained" by the white man that the South "shall be and remain a white man's country." "The consciousness of a function in these premises," he said, "whether expressed with the frenzy of a demagogue or maintained with a patrician's quietude, is the cardinal test of a Southerner and the central theme of southern history."

The search for monistic central themes is a quest that has attracted thinkers in all times, and one that seems to have a special fascination for students of the South, but it is also one that has been confounded repeatedly by the diversity of human experience, in the South as well as elsewhere. In its geography and history, in its society and economy, in its politics and ideology, the South has experienced a diversity that resists synthesis under any all-encompassing concept yet found, whether it be in some unfortunate phrase like "sowbelly and segregation" or in the grandiose schemes of romanticism, economic determinism, or the ideology of white supremacy—although each of these may throw considerable light upon the character and history of the South.

At the same time, however, it cannot be denied that a preoccupation with the issue of race, its mythology and its symbolism has been one of the major themes of southern history, with innumerable ramifications into

*George B. Tindall, "The Central Theme Revisited," in Charles Grier Sellers, Jr. (ed.), *The Southerner as American* (Chapel Hill, N.C.: University of North Carolina Press, 1960), pp. 104–112, 114–128. Footnotes omitted.

every aspect of southern life. Every Southerner of the present generation can recognize the continuing validity of James Weldon Johnson's observation in 1912 that "no group of Southern white men could get together and talk for sixty minutes without bringing up the 'race question.' If a Northern white man happened to be in the group, the time could be safely cut to thirty minutes."

But to speak of a preoccupation with issues of race is not to say that there is or ever has been a monolithic unity in the thought or practice of southern whites on the subject. For attitudes have ranged from the anti-slavery Negrophobia of Hinton Rowan Helper to the liberal equalitarianism of George Washington Cable. Nor can it be said that either the theory or social reality of race relations in the South has been constant. They have, in fact, gone through numerous changes: from the uncertain status of the first Negroes in early Virginia through the evolution of slavery, from the post-Revolutionary liberalism to the pro-slavery argument, from emancipation and Radical Reconstruction to Redemption and the rise of the twentieth-century system of white supremacy, and into accelerated change in the present generation.

Yet, underlying the diversity of southern experience, certain lines of continuity are apparent. Theory and practice with respect to race relations have moved chiefly in two broad channels developed in the eighteenth and nineteenth centuries. The first of these is what Gunnar Myrdal has labelled "the American Creed." It stems principally from the eighteenth-century philosophy of the rights of man, but has important sources also in Christianity and English law. The ideals "of the essential dignity of the individual human being, of the fundamental equality of all men, and of certain inalienable rights to freedom, justice, and a fair opportunity," says Myrdal, "represent to the American people the essential meaning of the nation's early struggle for independence.

The existence of these ideals, he maintains, has set up a tremendous ideological conflict, which he pictures as largely a psychological struggle within the individual who recognizes that racial prejudices and discriminatory practices do not conform to the generally accepted creed. But in the South, resistance to the "American Creed" has been bolstered by a counter creed which has supplied the white Southerner with racial sanctions that are somewhat more than the expression of individual racial prejudice.

If Myrdal's "American Creed" was primarily a product of the struggle for independence, then what Howard W. Odum has called the "credo of the South with reference to the Negro" was in large part the product of sectional conflict. Thrown on the defensive by the vigorous abolitionist assault of the 1830's, the southern leadership perfected an elaborate philosophical justification for the "peculiar institution" of slavery. Whether or not the masses of southern whites were aware of its existence, its influence was pervasive and they accepted most of its basic tenets.

Although the Civil War and Reconstruction shattered the institutional basis upon which race relations had rested in the South for more than two centuries, even this profound upheaval failed to undermine the prevailing patterns of thought on race—pro-slavery doctrines had penetrated too deeply into southern thinking. During the brief period when President Andrew Johnson was able to leave conservative whites in charge of southern state governments, most of them adopted more or less elaborate "black codes," which sought to retain as much white control over the civil and economic status of Negroes as the new conditions permitted.

As soon as the northern radicals established their dominance, however, the black codes were wiped out. It was now clear that the prevailing southern ideas on race would have to find new modes of social expression. By the time white southern Democrats secured control of their states in the 1870's, new constitutional amendments guaranteed certain rights to Negro citizens. The national Democratic party in 1872 announced its acceptance of these amendments as a *fait accompli*. And while the southern Democrats' rise to power had come about in campaigns characterized by the intimidation of Negroes, those campaigns and the Compromise of 1877 had also been accompanied by Democratic commitments to respect the newly-won legal rights of the freedman.

The Democratic Redeemers represented white supremacy, which they believed to be the supremacy of intelligence and character, but they also represented a measure of moderation that did not equate white supremacy as yet with Negro proscription. For a number of years, as Professor C. Vann Woodward has pointed out, certain forces operated as elements of restraint against the triumph of extreme racism. These forces were southern liberalism, a weak thing at best; northern liberalism and the threat of renewed intervention; the conservative spirit of the Redeemers; and the radicalism of the agrarian movement, which for a time united whites and Negroes in their common economic grievances.

With the collapse of these restraints in the 1890's, something endemic in southern thought asserted itself with new vehemence. Because of new circumstances and because of the Reconstruction amendments it found expression in new instrumentalities, but by the first decade of the twentieth century the main patterns of a new "peculiar institution" of white supremacy had become clear. These patterns embodied the now familiar forms of economic subordination, disfranchisement, segregation, and [political] proscription . . . [which] involved a return to conditions

roughly approximating those before emancipation. But the keystone of the whole new structure may be found in the caste symbolism of racial segregation. . . . Racial segregation as known in the twentieth century was not a necessary accompaniment of slavery, for that institution in itself provided the necessary symbols and instrumentalities of white supremacy. Segregation as a general civil institution and as a hallowed social myth is essentially a phenomenon of the twentieth century.

When the forces of white supremacy had completed their work, the product was remarkably similar in purpose and appearance to the slave codes of ante-bellum days, even more complex and thoroughgoing in application, yet different because of new circumstances and especially because of the Reconstruction amendments. If the Negroes' caste status could not be defined legally in terms of slavery or of laws with specific racial discriminations, it could be defined in terms of economic legislation, the establishment of restrictions upon the suffrage, and certain other formal restrictions under the convenient legal doctrine of "separate but equal" facilities, although segregation in practice seldom meant equal facilities and often involved the complete ostracism of Negroes from community activities.

Looking upon their work and finding it good, the authors of the new dispensation saw little need for developing new rationalizations. Rather they found that "Numerous theories, already well-worn in the ante-bellum period, were at hand to justify the caste system." These were the ingrained doctrines of the pro-slavery argument. The Scriptural justification of slavery, for example, reappeared in later years as an argument for discrimination and segregation. . . .

The economic justification of slavery similarly re-emerged in the contention that subordinated Negroes afforded a superior supply of "mud sill" labor. . . .

Some points of the pro-slavery argument were actually charged with added potency by postwar developments. In a variety of unpremeditated ways, the ante-bellum web of personal association between whites and Negroes broke down following emancipation. The tenant system disrupted the plantation community; residential segregation gradually came to be accepted as the natural pattern in the newer sections of southern towns and cities; a pattern of segregated schools was set by northern missionary agencies bent upon supplying the supposedly peculiar educational needs of a people newly freed from slavery; and Negroes found opportunities for independence and responsibility in their own separate churches. As the races drew apart and as opportunities for personal acquaintance, even in a paternalistic setting, diminished, the ante-bellum argument that the Negro was biologically distinct from and inferior to the white man gained an acceptance which had been prohibited during the slavery regime by the opposition of churchmen and by the more intimate knowledge of Negroes. . . .

Just as the institutional and personal estrangement of the races gave new currency to the biological inferiority argument, so the bitter controversies of the Reconstruction years, which were viewed largely as race conflicts, exacerbated the ante-bellum assumption of a fundamental antagonism of race. Even Jefferson had been frightened by the potentialities of race conflict if the restraints of slavery should be removed; and the appeal to social stability became one of the most potent weapons in the pro-slavery arsenal. . . .

White Southerners interpreted almost any exercise of the freedmen's new physical and social mobility as a bid for "social equality." The precise meaning of the term was uncertain, but the hypersensitivity of white men to the remotest suggestion of sexual relations between Negro men and white women charged it with overtones of fear. By the 1890's ambitious politicians were playing upon the frustrations generated by the agrarian depression to arouse against the helpless Negroes that old fear of racial conflict which had made rumors of Negro insurrection such a terror to the ante-bellum countryside.

How simple, then, to seize upon the principle of separation as a means of lessening the possibility of conflict and "amalgamation," at the same time making it a symbol of the Negroes' permanent subordination! Our scanty knowledge of the movement for segregation laws indicates that arguments for their passage emphasized most of all their contribution to public tranquility. . . . Whether uttered in terms of the potentialities of the situation or in terms of an agitator's threat, the danger of race conflict has been one of the chief justifications for white supremacy in its various forms.

In addition to theories derived from the pro-slavery argument, there were also certain new factors that could be called into the defense of white supremacy. Out of the sectional conflict there had arisen powerful symbols of Southernism: the romantic picture of the old plantation, the cult of the Confederacy and its heroes, and especially the memory of Reconstruction. By the turn of the century the great traumatic experience of Reconstruction was being rehearsed in ever more macabre terms by politicians, historians, and novelists. . . .

The new dispensation was not an institution clearly defined in law and in the minds of men, as slavery had been, but rather an ill-defined mélange of diverse factors of economic domination, repression by force and intimidation, political disfranchisement, segregation, and proscription either by private or public imposition. Nor was there any cohesive group like the old slaveholders whose leadership and immediate interests demanded eternal vigilance in the defense of their peculiar institution. The result was that the defense of white supremacy was never fully reformulated, but remained essentially the lengthened shadow of the pro-slavery argument.

Looking back over the first half of the twentieth century, it becomes clear that a whole series of developments was beginning imperceptibly to undermine the ideological defenses of white supremacy almost as soon as its new institutional patterns became established. The doctrine of biological inferiority was questioned by anthropologists and geneticists who could find no conclusive evidence for it, and their ideas seeped into the public consciousness. Tortured interpretations of the Scriptures were taken less and less seriously by literate Southerners. The need for a mudsill labor force was reduced by the development of mechanization in agriculture and industry. The argument for a separate Negro culture ran up against the manifest fact that Negroes could and did assimilate the general southern and American patterns, even in their separate institutions. The fear of race conflict with any relaxation of caste barriers eventually was found to be exaggerated as Negroes were re-enfranchised and segregation was ruled out in some areas without the predicted blood bath. And finally, these matters were opened up for discussion and debate in countless classrooms and organizations. . . .

In times of change it is only natural to look for new factors as explanations [that have contributed to the erosion of the ideological defense of white supremacy]. . . . Yet equally important was the traditionally ambiguous nature of the southern position, for it was this that made the new peculiar institution vulnerable to the twentieth-century challenges. The spell cast by the Southern Credo and the widespread assumption that it constitutes the central explanation of southern character have obscured the equally fundamental role of its antithesis, which in the larger

Southernism has been a continuing source of disquietude about the Southern Credo.

For while the American as Southerner has been unable to shake off the pro-slavery argument, the Southerner as American has never abandoned the American Creed. Southern liberals have repeatedly argued that the liberal traditions of American nationalism are to a considerable degree southern in their origins, and national heroes of southern birth like Jefferson and Jackson have been invoked to lend respectability to their views. . . .

If few ante-bellum Southerners could really assimilate the neofeudalism of the pro-slavery argument, fewer still could be found in the New South willing to attack frontally the valuations of the American Creed by attempting to build a general theory of society on a mudsill foundation, however implicit the idea may have been in their general outlook. Inhibited by moral taboos, Gunnar Myrdal has suggested, the Southerner has found it impossible to think *"constructively along segregation lines"* or "to think through carefully and in detail how a segregation system could be rationally organized. For *this would imply an open break with the principles of equality and liberty."* . . .

The changes already brought about by the effects of attack and criticism would seem to necessitate some re-examination of the widely-held view largely based upon the history of the nineteenth-century sectional conflict, that "outside" criticism weakens the forces of moderation within the South and generates nothing but intransigence, which in turn generates further criticism and so on into a deepening whirlpool.

Granting some force to this argument, it remains to be recognized that criticism has other effects in a libertarian society, especially when the criticized share many of the assumptions on which the criticism is based. Where those who are free from the pressures of the new peculiar institution have spoken or acted forcefully and judiciously, they have sometimes raised the problem to a level where conscious recognition of basic incongruities becomes inescapable. It is true that psychologists have recognized the possibility of an individual's holding several incompatible views at one and the same time, but Myrdal has suggested that "A need will be felt by the person or group, whose inconsistencies in valuations are publicly exposed, to find a means of reconciling the inconsistencies. This can be accomplished by adjusting one of the conflicting pairs of valuations. Thus criticism of southern racial practice has repeatedly generated temporary intransigence, but in the long run and more significantly it has also compelled self-justification and a slow but steady adjustment by white Southerners in the direction of the American faith in equality of opportunity and rights.

This is, in part, evidence of the lasting victory of those earlier critics who wrote the fourteenth and fifteenth amendments into the Constitution. While there have been dire predictions of violence and bloodshed to come from any tampering with southern folkways, there has been a widespread acceptance of Negro suffrage in places where it would have been unthinkable a generation ago. Political leaders, even in the midst of growing tensions (and perhaps because of them), talk increasingly in terms of equal facilities and opportunities. Measures of segregation have generally been defended under the legal fiction of "separate but equal" facilities; and where the attack has come white leaders have generally capitulated to a movement to give at least a semblance of reality to the principle of equality. Whereas in 1940 a Gallup poll showed that about half of the white Southerners frankly opposed "equal" education for Negroes, today even the segregationist leadership avows equality as its goal and has taken important steps towards it.

This has been a truly profound change in the thinking of white Southerners, albeit somewhat obscured in the blood and thunder of newspaper headlines.

In emphasizing the significance of the American Creed and the pressures brought in its name, it is not intended to say that changes in southern thought and action have been brought about only by the operation of outside forces, for criticism has also originated in the South, nor can it be said that the South is a peculiar repository of the eighteenth-century Enlightenment. Other traditional factors have persisted with equal or greater tenacity in the South and have imparted a distinctive flavor to its culture and heritage.

One of the factors has been Christianity. "Conservatism in religion," one historian holds, "did not rank far behind traditional racial attitudes as significant causes for the South's retention of its regional distinctiveness. The effect of the social gospel movement has undoubtedly been a factor in the advanced pronouncements of major southern church bodies on issues of race. Yet the southern churches, on the whole, have remained wedded to orthodoxy in spite of cynical jibes at the "Bible Belt." One result of this has been a deep-seated moral-religious consciousness that has always proved troublesome to the Southern Credo from the day of primitive anti-slavery among backwoods Methodists and Baptists to the day of the outstanding practitioner of contemporary evangelism, a native Southerner who has sought and has had unsegregated audiences at his meetings in the South. . . .

The churches have never been the spearhead of social change in the South, it is true. "With all its mighty influence," said Howard Odum, "the power of the church has been in its ideologies and conditioning attitudes and not in its program." But these ideologies and conditioning attitudes have, with few exceptions, functioned as an important restraint upon the most extreme expressions of racism, and have thereby contributed importantly to the erosion of the Southern Credo.

Not only the church, but also the lingering influence of frontier and agrarian society, have contributed to that "exaggerated individualism" which W. J. Cash found to be one of the essential characteristics of the Southerner. Respect for the individual personality and a certain easy-going "personalness" in human relations have continued to carry a significance in the South that has not been wholly undermined by the encroachments of industry or urbanism. . . .

The neighborly spirit of human relations in the South also has democratic as well as aristocratic implications, stemming in some measure from the historical influence of frontier and agrarian democracy that has been as much a part of the southern tradition as the feudal heritage of the plantation. In the southern experience recognition of a community of interest between whites and Negroes has been manifested by individuals and groups other than those with pretensions to gentility. During any period in southern history since the Civil War some instances of interracial action may be found in the labor movement, among craftsmen, longshoremen, miners, factory workers, and others. In the agrarian revolt of the eighties and nineties the "wool hat boys" found themselves allied with Negro farmers in the struggle against their common economic grievances, and since the nineteen-thirties an indigenous organization of tenant farmers and agricultural laborers has existed without racial barriers. Middle-class manifestations of a community of interest have appeared in various projects for community improvement such as Community Chest drives. . . .

Last of all, the intellectual and economic progress of Negroes has nurtured the seeds of change by developing Negro institutions and enterprises and professional occupations, with leaders dependent upon the Negro community and relatively independent of white control. Such leadership has frequently provided the spearhead of the most effective actions against discrimination, sometimes through tactics of adjustment and at other times through tactics of protest and criticism. . . .

A gradual diminution in the force of the Southern Credo has now been apparent for several decades. Though persisting in most of its aspects, the new peculiar institution itself began to show signs of strain under pressure in the thirties, in the forties it began to crack, and . . . , in the fifties, its chief symbol and support, Jim Crow, has come under virtual sentence of death by the federal courts. The threatened collapse of any institution, however, may bring forth a stubborn defense. Hostile reactions to civil rights programs and especially to the Supreme Court decision in the school segregation cases demonstrate that the old ideas are held with remarkable tenacity. They have even experienced a certain revival, born in the late nineteen-thirties and mounting to a peak of intensity in the fifties.

This new reaction invites comparison with the defense of slavery. The white Citizens' Councils and similar groups, for example, had their counterpart in the vigilance committees of the Old South. Some political spokesmen of the white South have revived the dormant ante-bellum theory of nullification in a new form. Other segregationist leaders— like the secessionists of Charleston, who "adopted as an article of faith the propagation of slavery" with all the zeal of "the Mormons or early Mahometans"—have sought to erect the temporary *modus vivendi* of segregation into some kind of eternal moral principle. Analogies of the sort could be pursued at great length, but at several important points the comparison breaks down.

In the first place, the slavery interests of the eighteen-fifties were to some extent on the offensive, actively seeking the extension of slavery into the territories. The tone of the new reaction is decidedly defensive, seeking only to hold the ground already occupied, or even to retreat to the line of separate but equal.

In the second place, the oratory and literature of the new reaction have shown no serious promise of developing a positive philosophical justification of the new peculiar institution. An intellectual leadership of the sort that perfected the pro-slavery argument is conspicuous by its absence. Such efforts at rationalization as have appeared lean heavily upon charging the opposition with questionable motives and susceptibility to insidious influences. This observation may seem to place an excessive emphasis upon the rationality of human motivation in an area where irrationality has often ruled. Yet the lack of a reasoned defense may very well constitute a serious long-range vulnerability of an institution that conflicts with so many values deeply imbedded in the traditions and thought of the people.

In the third place, the solid front of southern whites in the eighteen-fifties has been splintered in the nineteen-fifties. What George Washington Cable once called the "Silent South" is now articulate. Church organizations, citizens' groups, individuals, even prominent political leaders have demonstrated publicly their indifference or hostility to the old Southern Credo. Assertion of the American Creed in the face of serious pressures makes it difficult to assume that the old spell of unanimity will ever be revived. Even spokesmen for the new reaction seem in many cases to have adopted in private the attitude, which sometimes crops out in public utterances, that their function is in the nature of a rear guard delaying action rather than a lasting revival of white supremacy doctrines.

Adequate appraisal of contemporary developments is an uncertain business. But one southern historian has been "so bold as to

maintain that recent changes are of sufficient depth and impact as to define the end of an era of Southern history." If the dynamics of recent events can inspire so bold an observation, they must also lead us to consider whether we may be witnessing the disappearance of the South as a conscious entity.

For if we accept the analysis of U. B. Phillips, that day when white supremacy should be no longer the cardinal tenet and primary aim of white Southerners would be the day in which the South would become but another geographical part of the United States, for the central theme of its history and the chief source of its unity would have come to an end. It would be a rash prophet indeed who would forecast when that day might come, but in view of general trends over the past three decades and the direction of public policy today, it can no longer seem so completely outside the range of possibility as it must have seemed to Phillips in 1928.

But would a decline and fall of white supremacy necessarily reduce the South to merely another geographical part of the United States? Only if we must accept the dictum of Phillips that white supremacy is the central and indispensable determinant of southern peculiarity. Though for a century and a half the issue of race has been an important key to southern character and one of the chief issues on which other elements of Southernism and Americanism have interacted, we cannot in the light of recent events continue to regard it as an immutable feature of southern life.

Present perspectives suggest, indeed, that the "credo of the South with reference to the Negro" can no longer be regarded as the indispensable key to southern distinctiveness— just as, for that matter, the American Creed fails to explain fully the broader national character. The Southern Credo has never summarized the diverse aspects of the southern heritage. This is recognized in popular thought, for popular stereotypes of the

Southerner have flourished and have been readily recognized without any overt reference to the issue of race. Southerners themselves have time and again manifested intense regional loyalties in situations dissociated from an emphasis on the issue of race—the cotton mill campaign of the 1880's, for example, the Southern Education Movement around the turn of the century, the campaign against freight rate discrimination, the Agrarian manifesto of 1930, and the development of an academic ideology of southern regionalism by Howard W. Odum and his disciples.

The historian can report, too, that the Negro has been a Southerner. The point is seldom comprehended in the general usage of the term "Southerner," but the records and literature of the South bear voluminous recognition of the fact. In making the culture of the South, W. J. Cash asserted, "Negro entered into white man as profoundly as white man entered into Negro—subtly influencing every gesture, every word, every emotion and idea, every attitude." In shaping patterns of speech, of folklore, of music, of literature, and in the manifold products of their labor, Negro Southerners have everlastingly influenced and enriched the culture of their region. To overlook this contribution would be to neglect much that has made the South distinctive. . . .

Finally, we return to U. B. Phillips' central theme of southern history. To recognize the Negro as a Southerner is perhaps to deliver the *coup de grâce* to the Phillips thesis, but before abandoning it precipitately, we must render a proper deference to its great validity in explaining much about the South. Phillips' essay dealt chiefly with the antebellum South and in that context it emphasized the importance of slavery, as a race issue, in forging that consciousness of southern unity which culminated in secession and the Confederacy. It was reprinted, most appropriately, at the end of a volume entitled *The Course of the South to Secession*. At the

time of Phillips' writing it was an interpretation that was losing favor in many quarters, but more recent historians like Allan Nevins and Arthur M. Schlesinger, Jr., have tended to turn back to slavery and racism as the fundamental issue in their explanations of the sectional controversy and Civil War.

In this essay, however, we have tried to view the subject in a broader context than politics, which Phillips scarcely did, and also in the perspective of a New South now older than the Old South ever was while it existed. In this perspective a larger Southernism is an unquestionable reality, especially to those who have grown up in the South, and the historian can list some of the objective factors that produced it: a distinctive historical experience involving defeat and poverty; the climate and physical setting with their effects on life, tempo, emotion, and character; the presence of the Negro and his pervasive influence on the whole life of the region; the powerful religious heritage and the knowledge of good and evil; and finally, the persistence of an essentially rural culture with its neighborliness in human relations.

Yet the historian who is also a Southerner knows that the reality of Southernism—like so many important aspects of experience—defies precise definition or objective analysis. This reality he knows best as a Southerner, for whom it is a subjective experience of land and people and ways of living, which has become a ground for attachment and loyalty. As an historian he can only report that the many different kinds of people living in the South's many widely different parts find a large degree of common meaning in their infinitely various personal experiences.

He can report, in short, that the southern way of life has involved infinitely more than a system of segregation and proscription. And more and more frequently, as time passes, he can report that a consciousness of loyalty to the South may even take the form of opposition to the old Southern Credo.

The South was changing dramatically by mid-twentieth century, and one of the most perceptive historians in discerning the new conditions has been THOMAS D. CLARK (b. 1903), for many years chairman of the department of history at the University of Kentucky and now Distinguished Professor at Indiana University. Analyzing the swift changes in a book entitled *The Emerging South* (1961), Clark describes the altered relationships of the races in the unsettled times following World War II. Other volumes on the New South by Clark include *Pills, Petticoats and Plows: The Southern Country Store* (1944), *The Southern Country Editor* (1948), *Three Paths to the Modern South* (1965), and (with Albert D. Kirwan) *The South Since Appomattox: A Century of Regional Change* (1967).*

Thomas D. Clark

The Challenge of Desegregation

If a modern Olmsted, Tocqueville, or Archer traveled through the present South he would hear observations southerners were making a century ago, and he doubtless would hear the same social philosophy given expression. Even in this period of transition from agriculture to industry, and from a predominantly rural society to an expanding urbanism, the Negro remains a central theme of southern life. When the modern southerner speaks so vehemently about maintaining the southern way of life, he is not talking about old economic or regional folk patterns, for these have almost vanished; he has in mind one specific subject—racial relations.

In another way the Negro influence in the South has made itself felt. In the last decade and a half not one session of a legislature in the ex-slave states has failed to give the Negro serious attention. In fact, so much attention has been given this subject that many times lawmakers have overlooked other vital legislation. Even special sessions of legislatures have been called to consider the subject. No one will ever know how much committee meetings, interstate conferences, and the communication of all sorts of political groups have cost the South in dollars and cents. If this were spent in combating tuberculosis it would go far to eradicate the disease.

In a less formal way the Negro theme has colored casual conversations. One can scarcely spend an evening in the South without hearing it discussed. Less well-

---

*From *The Emerging South* by Thomas D. Clark. Copyright © 1961 by Thomas D. Clark. Reprinted by permission of Oxford University Press, Inc. Pp. 206–225. The title "The Challenge of Desegregation" has been supplied by the editor.

informed persons inject it into conversations in the form of anxious questions. They reveal both their fears and their prejudices in these questions. Some discussions reflect lack of confidence in a large part of the southern population itself to maintain racial integrity. Newspapers, regional periodicals, religious and educational publications, books, pamphlets, and broadsides all reflect the deep concern of the South with the place of the Negro in regional society.

A visitor coming to the South for the first time might get the impression that a powerful minority of people in the region with strong leadership capacity was bringing about a social renaissance. He would look for the driving force in the new industrialism for an explanation. He might reason that a fresh wave of democracy following World War II and the responsibilities of free-world leadership by the United States had created this condition. A better informed individual might reach the conclusion that the South arrived at its present stage of racial dilemma at a most unfortunate moment in its history. Not only does it face the enormous challenges wrought by changes in its general economic structure, but also by changes in social and political conditions in many parts of the world. Although the arguments of southern Senators and the reactions of southerners generally are against the Court in this trying moment, the external pressures, whether from northern politicians, the organized Negro, regional critics in general, or from undefined sources, are infinitely greater. They stem from the vast struggle for survival of the free world itself. If the basis of the present racial confusion were purely regional, then the solutions would be less complex, but it is not. This fact depresses the southerner more than he is able to express.

It would indeed be a sad mistake to consider the race problem in the South purely in the light of its current painful state. Many people of course considered slavery a paradox in a democratic society. However, it was the fatal lack of planning for the rehabilitation of the ex-slave following the Civil War that produced one of America's major social tragedies. However humane and astute the Lincoln Administration was, it did not provide properly for the freedom of the Negro. Even the most ardent abolitionist crusaders failed to deal with this important and vital problem. The whole process of reconstruction in which the Negro was used as a social and political pawn was a further tragedy. After reconstruction ended, ambitious politicians made use of him. He was largely disenfranchised, for, then as now, southern politicians preferred to deal with the smallest number of voters rather than try to sway large masses.

The troubled South compounded the difficulty in the years after reconstruction by allowing the horrible practice of lynching to become widespread. It was not countless victims of rope and fagot who suffered but rather the South's honor, self-respect, and peace of mind. No community which ever experienced a lynching could then say that it was morally or spiritually better off the next day. The deeper the South got into the brutal practice, the guiltier became the regional conscience. The South was caught in a trap from which it had great difficulty extricating itself, for lynching brought down upon it bitter criticism from all parts of the world. Even southern morals and Christianity were challenged; in general the region was put very much on the defensive. Lynching bred fear of possible Negro retaliation, which in turn was one of the basic excuses for the practice. But, deeper was the fear of a breakdown of the Anglo-Saxon system of justice, which in the long run would affect white southerners even more than Negroes.

An almost negligible number of southerners either committed or condoned lynching, but it was not the guilty individual who stood convicted. The South as a region was adjudged guilty, guilty at the doors of the governors, the legislatures, the courts, and the law-enforcement officers. No clear-thinking southerner who stood beneath a swaying body suspended from the limb of a tree and read the dangling placard inscribed with bitter hatred could excuse the act. Lynching was a savage act in the light of every tenet of the Christian way of life, and of every principle of an established system of justice. Repeatedly southern representatives opposed federal anti-lynching legislation, not because they condoned the act, but because they realized their political future depended on such a stand. In a less selfish way they realized that such legislation would charge the South officially with sinning against the laws of humanity.

Gradually the South has stemmed the crime of lynching. Southerners emphasize this fact when they attempt to show how the South was making headway in solving its race problems even before 1954. But the South is not given such great credit for halting this practice, for people outside the region and elsewhere in the world have looked upon lynching as such a gross form of lawlessness and violence that it never should have been countenanced in the first place. And even today the practice has not been completely wiped out. The lynching of Mack Charles Parker at Poplarville, Mississippi, on April 26, 1959, shocked people everywhere. Newspapers carried the story emblazoned in bold headlines. The failure to bring the murderers to justice made nonsoutherners doubt the efficacy of southern progress in this area.

Changes wrought by World War II were of tremendous importance to the postwar South. Not only was the Negro called upon to do his part at home and in the armed forces, and not only was he told that he was a full beneficiary of the advantages of a democratic society in which he lived, but he was helped by the emotional racist campaign of Nazism, which the American government was actively combating. Parallel to this was the rising world resistance to colonialism unleashed by the war. This anticolonial movement was directed not only against imperialism but against discrimination against minorities; indeed, the two were equated by the newly emergent powers. It has been the United States Government, not the South or a single state, which has had to answer these charges when they have been leveled against either the South or the nation as a whole. In answering these charges of discrimination and colonialism the Government has incurred the wrath of southern extremists as well as the gibes of the new nations which raised the issues. Thus the South finds itself suddenly caught in an international net which it had not known existed.

For the southern Negro the changing world situation has had deep implications. For the first time his position as a minority person has been emphasized, and he has found powerful world support from other minority groups, who have asked many embarrassing questions of a nation trying desperately hard to maintain a foreign policy which professes a point of view favorable to the protection of minority rights. Thus the cause of the southern Negro suddenly becomes a national issue involving the delicate balance of the United States before a free world.

On the local domestic scene one of the most confusing of all issues was the "place" of the Negro in southern society. His position in the regional social system was poorly defined from the beginning, but, as years passed, it became a more highly restrictive one. This was especially true as Jim Crow laws and folk customs forced him into a perpetual condition of retreat. Modern social relocation of the Negro in the South has helped shatter the old folk pattern, a fact which has done great violence to the old ways of life.

The issue of status is important in the South's present racial turmoil. Once the

Negro's position was defined by a casual and indifferent social relationship with the white man which involved every aspect of his life. The white man seldom bothered to define the bounds of the Negro's place. In some instances they were broad, and in others they were extremely narrow, but whatever they were, they were exercised in day-to-day personal relationships. Once these were disrupted, the Negro turned to the federal courts and the Constitution for a more precise definition of his place, not in a community nor in relationships with specific white men, but in a democracy and a world society. The courts have been more specific in their definitions in this area than the old system could have ever tolerated. The old casualness has been destroyed, and in its place has been substituted the force of law and its interpretation.

Since 1945 there has been a systematic effort to lower discriminatory barriers in areas where Jim Crow laws bound the Negro's freedom of social action in the older South. The first important area in which this has been done is at the polls. Negro leadership knows full well that its toughest fight is to gain full and accepted rights to participate freely in politics in the South. The race has a long, bitter history behind it in the ordeal of exercising its right to vote. It knows the well-nigh insurmountable legal barriers which presently bar Negroes from the polls in some states, or the numerous clever subterfuges which can turn them out the side door without the ballot. Their great-grandfathers learned almost all of these things when they were victimized by both radical Republicans and defiant white southerners in the fight to control the southern vote during the reconstruction era.

The Negro remembers the bitter struggle over his voting franchise in those grim days of the subsequent Populist crusade. He knows intimately what Theodore G. Bilbo meant in Mississippi, in the first round in the courts

over white primaries, when he said that if the circuit clerks of Mississippi did not know how to keep the Negroes from registering then he could show them. On the other hand southern politicians were not oblivious to the fact that admission of Negroes to the polls would bring their careers to abrupt ends. Doubtless the whole approach to the voters in the campaign in the South would be diametrically changed if the Negro voted. A good contrast is that between political campaigns in Kentucky and Georgia. A Kentucky politician shouting racial defiance from the stump would only be hastening his defeat. In September 1959 the two gubernatorial candidates in Kentucky were quick to shout "No!" to a Centre College student's question of whether or not they would favor closing the public schools rather than integrating them. This was in sharp contrast to attitudes expressed by candidates in the Georgia and Mississippi gubernatorial campaigns.

Sometime in the future the Negro, after a massive amount of civil rights legislation, commission investigation, platform writing by the two parties, and court action, will finally remove barriers to his voting. However, he has a tremendous handicap to overcome. First, the mass of southern Negroes must be educated at least to the extent that they can pass a moderate high school test in citizenship. It will not be sufficient defense for the Negro to point out that literally thousands of white voters fall far below the standards set for Negro voters, for it is he who is faced with the fight to gain the right to vote. One of the most difficult issues is the educational requirements for registration. There may be no objection to setting an educational requirement at a level in keeping with national educational attainment of the mass of the population, but if it is used for discriminatory purposes then it is being prostituted.

Before the Negro in general reaches the stage where he can exert an appreciable in fluence at the polls, he will have to generate enough interest among his people to get large numbers of them to undergo the exasperations of registering and then of appearing at the polls to cast their votes. The Negro not only shares the southern white man's apathy toward voting, but he suffers from an ingrained fear of white retribution toward "smart" Negroes who insist on voting.

An impartial observer in the present South could hardly fail to sense that it is only by gaining access to the polls that the Negro can hope to make more rapid progress as a free and competitive citizen. Desegregation of public schools is by comparison of secondary importance. Whether or not the schools are desegregated now or at some unforeseeable date in the future, however, does not mean that the Negro will stand still educationally. But until he gains full access to the polls and uses this right he obviously will stand still politically.

In erecting barriers to the Negro's registering and voting, extremist southerners are possibly doing more than any other Americans to hasten the day when he will vote. This was implicit in Governor John Battle's plea with the Alabama registration officials in December 1959 to deliver the Macon County voter records. For while public opinion in the nation might be somewhat reluctant to push desegregation of the public school system faster than wise and lasting adjustments can be made, hardly anyone outside the South would look favorably upon the attempt to keep free Americans away from the polls, no matter what their social or educational background. Repeatedly this argument was made in the civil rights debate in the United States Senate, both in 1957 and 1960. Senators who were not as emotionally aroused over the legal technicalities of the pending bill in 1957 as were some partisans on both sides of the great debate reiterated the point of view that the ballot must be kept free. Senator

Edward Thye of Minnesota, for instance, in querying Senator John McClellan of Arkansas, said, "It is late Saturday afternoon, and here on the floor of the Senate my concern is that every American citizen shall have equal rights as a citizen. I care not of what race, color, or creed he may be. That is the first point. The first premise of my public service is to try to make possible that each one share in the blessedness of this government equally with all others." The right to vote has come to be considered an inherent right of a free people, and before the world court of public opinion Americans cannot refrain from accepting the proposition that all their people are free.

It is one of the anomalies of American politics that while the Negro, slave and free, has been a basic political issue in the South since the adoption of the Missouri Compromise in 1820, his vote has rarely had any real consequence except during reconstruction. This has been especially true in areas where the Negro population has greatly outnumbered the white. Yet the Negro has disturbed both the polls and legislative halls as a troubled ghost of the American democratic system. He has never been present in spirit in greater and more disturbing force than in the great debate over civil rights in the United States Senate in the hot summer of 1957 and again in February 1960. In the lengthy debates, Senator Paul Douglas of Illinois accused Senator Russell Long of Louisiana, and southerners in general, of being victims of a Freudian guilt complex.

On July 13, Senator John McClellan discussed what might be considered one of the central issues so far as the southern opposition was concerned. He said, "This bill has been advanced primarily to affect the protection of voting rights. But this bill will affect a far wider field, and whether it is intentional or not, this bill would have a terrific impact on the problem of integrating the schools."

Later he said, "Thus, under the doctrine of the Brown case, if a Negro could show that two or more persons conspired to refuse or prohibit or prevent his attendance at an integrated public school, he could sue either one of them or both of them for damages. That is the law, that is one of the results of the Supreme Court's decision in the Brown case." Senator McClellan believed that under the proposed act the Attorney General of the United States could file an application for an injunction at the opening of schools, and that, "on the first day of school, if the situation had not been taken care of, a number of fine citizens would either be subject to being brought into court and arbitrarily tried, fined, and sent to jail for contempt of such a court order."

In the debate the southerners presented long and legalistic discussions of the development of trial by jury. The better informed lawyers among them spent considerable time discussing the technicalities of contempt offenses against the law in equity. The earlier debates became so involved in historical and legal phraseology that the right to vote was almost overlooked. However, the nub of the whole debate, despite the offending Section III, which threatened removal in vote-denial cases of the right of trial by jury, was whether or not Negroes were allowed to exercise freely the right to vote in all of the southern states. If Negro rights were denied, would southern white juries, upon the presentation of such facts, find for the plaintiffs?

On July 8, 1957, in the midst of the first debate, Senator Richard B. Russell of Georgia was challenged on a C.B.S. public affairs program by a reporter, who wanted to know whether it was true that when an all-white jury was voting on the rights of a Negro voter the latter had little chance of winning. Senator Russell replied, "Well, that's one of the common slanders that's been repeated against the South without a word of evidence to substantiate it. You have got a number of

criminal statutes on your books now where it is made a violation of criminal law, punishable by imprisonment and fine to interfere with the voting rights of any citizen. Now the South is entitled to have at least some proof brought forward of this charge that it is repeatedly bandied that every southern white man is so irresponsible that he would forswear himself or perjure himself in a case involving a Negro citizen."

The Georgia senator further maintained that there was no difficulty involved in his home state about the Negro's voting. He said, "I deny the statement as to voting. At least, as far as the greater portion of the South is concerned, there is no real limitation or restriction on the rights of qualified Negroes to vote." The issue of this statement might center on a definition of the word "qualified." It was this point to which Senator Douglas addressed himself on July 26 when he published in the Congressional *Record* a summary of Negro voting in the South made by the Southern Regional Council. This did not take sharp issue with Senator Russell's statements, but it did discuss the arduous and disheartening course which Negroes in many southern counties had to pursue to become qualified voters, and their responsibilities for keeping their names on the voter rolls after they were registered.

In this connection, the editor of the Colfax *Chronicle* of Grant Parish, Louisiana, on October 12, 1956, made a rather astounding observation. He said that members of the local Citizens Council had re-examined the voter rolls and had removed the names of many Negro voters. The president of the local Council, W. J. B. Jones, was reported to have said that his group voted unanimously to purge Negro voters, and an estimate was made that 90 per cent of the Negro registrants were challenged. The *Chronicle's* editor checked the first 100 white registrants' cards and found only one that would meet the exacting standards set for Negroes. He reported that not a single member of the Citizens Council committee had filled out his card correctly by the Council's standards.

Some states have used clever subterfuges to prevent the registration of Negro voters or to disqualify large blocks of voters once they are registered. In February 1959, the Associated Press reported that some Louisiana officials had plans under way to remove the names of over 100,000 people from the voting rolls of that state, but State Senator W. R. Rainach was reported as having said that, "Many would-be Negro voters would be eliminated for each white person affected." The device suggested would start with a long and complicated application form which applicants would be required to complete without help or benefit of notes and in their own handwriting. The second hurdle would be a request for applicants to interpret any section of the Louisiana or United States constitutions which the registrars might select, and the registrars in turn would judge whether or not applicants had interpreted the constitution correctly. Any mistake in form or fact would subject the applicant to disqualification and would prevent his name from being inscribed on the voting rolls. Future challengers would be empowered to scrutinize the applications of successful registrants for possible errors which had been overlooked. This sort of device is a ready-made one for arousing a widespread national opinion hostile to the South, and one which inevitably will lead to the enactment of sterner federal civil-rights legislation. The Commission on Civil Rights reported that the *Manual of Procedure for Registrars of Voters* carried a foreword which attacked the NAACP and its attempt to increase the registration of Negro voters. Its "Key to Victory" said, "We are in a life and death struggle with the Communists and the NAACP to maintain segregation and to preserve the liberties of our people. The impartial enforcement of our laws is the KEY TO VICTORY in this struggle."

In Georgia there was considerable reaction to the NAACP's threat to register three million Negro voters in the South. Numerous legislative means for preventing the registration of Negro voters have been proposed. If the present voter registration measures were strictly enforced, few people, white or black, educated or illiterate, would be able to register. In some instances registration laws do little more than suspend a legal axe over voters' heads. Individual applications can be reviewed as often in the future as challengers might wish to do so. Characteristic of some of this legislation was that outlined in 1957 by representative Peter Zack Geer of Colquitt County, Georgia. This proposal ultimately became the basis for the revised Georgia registration law. The law placed the right to vote largely in the field of social behavior. Prospective voters would be barred if they were parents of illegitimate children or parties to common-law marriages, or were accused of child abandonment or of possessing and transporting moonshine liquor, had failed to register or report for military service, had been adjudged guilty of bigamy, adultery, false swearing, or of committing a felony. Mr. Geer was said to have commented that 90 per cent of the adult Negroes of Georgia were guilty of adultery or bigamy, and 30 per cent were guilty of liquor violations. Besides these moral questions, applicants for voter registration would be asked thirty content questions which would range from, "What is the definition of a felony under Georgia Law?" to "What does the Constitution of the United States provide regarding the right of a citizen to vote?" A full answer to the latter question might incriminate the whole procedure.

The main feature of the Civil Rights Act of 1957 was the provision for the creation of a Commission on Civil Rights to "investigate allegations in writing as under oath or affirmation that certain citizens of the United States are being deprived of their right to vote and have that vote counted by reason of color, race, religion, or national origin." The Commission was instructed to collect information on vote discrimination, and to appraise the laws and policies of the Federal Government as to equal protection of the laws under the Constitution. Within two years the Commission was to report its findings and recommendations to the President and Congress. This Commission soon began holding hearings on alleged violations of voting rights in the South.

Judge Walter Geer of Colquitt County Superior Court threatened to jail Federal Bureau of Investigation agents and other federal investigators if they persisted in their efforts to examine voter records. Registrars and other voter officials were instructed not to allow federal investigators to see voting lists. Judge Geer said he believed the Terrell County suit, the first filed under the 1957 Civil Rights Act, was "arrogant, unwarranted, and high-handed."

A second case was filed against the registrars of Macon County, Alabama, and in turn against the State of Alabama in February 1959. In the Alabama case Judge Frank M. Johnson, Jr., held that the Federal Civil Rights Law was not broad enough to apply to the prosecution of a state for its violation. In the Terrell County case argued before Judge T. Hoys Davis, the court held that the law was so broad as to be considered unconstitutional. Thus two cases were sent to higher courts which took diametrically opposite points of view toward the effect of the Civil Rights Act of 1957.

The *Report* of the Civil Rights Commission in 1959 is an enlightening document which sets out much of the problem of removing barriers to voters in several of the southern states. In 1959 the Commission reported on three aspects of the problem of civil rights. These were voting, education and housing. It found that to a large extent discrimination in these fields was of a racial

nature. There was only one exception where vote denial was not "by reason of race or color." Heart of the Civil Rights Commission *Report* is the observation that "prejudice will not be cured by concentrating constantly on the discrimination. It may be cured, or reduced, or at least forgotten, if sights can be raised to new and challenging targets. Thus a curriculum designed to educate young Americans for this unfolding twentieth-century world, with better teachers and better schools, will go a long way to facilitate the transition of public education. Equal opportunity in housing will come more readily as part of a great program of urban reconstruction and regeneration. The right to vote will more easily be secured throughout the whole South if there are great issues on which people want to vote."

The Civil Rights Act of 1960 did not stir up quite as much furor in Congress, but at the same time it was far milder in the form passed by the House of Representatives than was the earlier act with its Point III section. The new law made three major provisions: (1) educational facilities in federal installations were to be desegregated; (2) bombings of schools and churches were made a federal offense; (3) in places where Negroes found it either too difficult or impossible to register, federal registrars would be appointed to register voters who wished to vote in federal elections. This law solves only a part of the registration problem and actually does little toward insuring the right to vote. There is a tremendous gulf between being registered to vote and actually voting. The new law still leaves room for all sorts of intimidation and subterfuge.

Participation in the political affairs of the South is possibly one of the most important goals which the Negro might hope to achieve. His achievement of this goal, however, makes greater demands on him educationally than is made of the white man. He has to erase as many of the old prejudices against him as possible in the shortest time. The idea has persisted for generations, aided by a defective educational system, that he is incapable of making political decisions. Education is after all the only means by which he may hope to achieve his free political rights, or to compete in the race for industrial jobs in the South.

The new southern industrial employer cannot afford to tolerate ignorance and illiteracy among his employees. One mistake on the part of a laborer in a plant might consume a considerable block of profits, if not endanger the lives and property of the entire labor force and plant. Whatever industrial management's philosophy of wages might be, it is certainly not that of the old agricultural landlord. No allowances are made in a highly competitive business for the wastes and inefficiencies customary in the old way of life. The new southern industry, like industry everywhere, must concern itself with efficiency in production if it is to compete successfully in the market places.

The new southern industrialism has brought promise of greater change in the area of demands on labor than in any other field. Since the opening of the nineteenth century, the South has been content to accept an adverse ratio of culture and efficiency level from that maintained by people in some of the other sections of the country. Consequently southerners have long accepted the humiliation of unfavorable social and cultural statistics as a matter of course. They have shrugged off the great social imbalance by saying that the low position of the South in numerous standards of measurement was due to the large Negro population. But now that the new industry has made certain social and cultural demands on the South, the region can no longer afford to let this element of the population set a regional standard.

The southern Negro's economic condition has changed radically. He, in fact, has often to demonstrate a greater competence than a white applicant for a job in order to overcome racial prejudice against him. Thus education suddenly has become his fundamental means of moving from the old economic system into the new. Again the Negro's crusade for better opportunities has the support of a general world struggle to control men's minds. His cause is helped by the near panic at this point for advancing American educational efforts at all levels, and by the fact that national safety itself is involved in educational progress of all the American people. So for the southern Negro the equality of educational opportunity has far more meaning than the mere matter of social desegregation. It carries with it a heavier responsibility, and demands greater effort of him than of past generations of his race. He has to wipe away by achievement the fixed notion that he is incapable of meeting the challenge of the white man's society.

The modern Negro in the South is called upon to have enormous patience. Scarcely a month goes by that he does not see or hear himself abused by someone in the public press, on the radio, or in the handbills and pamphlets which peddle racial hatred. Every opening session of the public schools drags him before the public, and frequently he is labeled an inferior person incapable of improving himself. Charges are sometimes made that he is being misled by the Communists and Communist-front organizations. The charge of Communist infiltration into the NAACP [National Association for the Advancement of Colored People] has been disproved. In his book *Masters of Deceit*, FBI Director J. Edgar Hoover has a clear-cut statement on this issue.

In this era of change, with emotions running so high, it is difficult to assess with any degree of accuracy the full impact of the race issue on the region's future. Two facts, however, seem to stand out beyond reasonable challenge. The Negro has as secure a place in the history of the South as does the white man, and he is in the South to stay. It is true, of course, that large numbers of Negroes migrate annually to other sections of the country, but this does not mean that they are deserting the South as a race.

Southern cultural history bears the deep stamp of both slave and free Negro. Sectional economics have been largely conditioned by Negro labor, and regional humor and folk culture have been enriched by the imaginative language and customs of the Negro. Religious reactions have reflected the fact that the Negro too has a soul worthy of salvation. The physical organization of the early churches took this fact into consideration. In fact the whole moral code of the South was long ago shaped to include the Negro, if for no other reason than that of preserving law and order. In a more fundamental way southern white and Negro lives have developed a common interest, and the two races have a common regional sentimentality.

Many white southerners have long assumed that they have an inborn understanding of the Negro. It is a novel thing indeed that many white men are quick to declare that they understand the Negro, while it is a rare occasion when a Negro will boast that he understands the white man. In fact the Negro's precise knowledge of his white neighbors is perhaps many folds greater than is white understanding of the Negro. Oftentimes this constant protestation of understanding closely resembles whistling past a darkened social graveyard. The plain truth perhaps is that few or no white southerners truly understand their Negro neighbors. Often individuals claim knowledge of the race, but a closer examination reveals that it is based on little more than associations with Negroes on a single farm or with household servants.

Human understanding involves a large number of factors, including knowledge of personality traits and innermost emotions and a sharing of ideas and beliefs and troubles and disappointments. Above all, it means a thoroughgoing intellectual honesty must

come into play. Southerners know that large numbers of Negroes nearly always put the best possible interpretation on situations when discussing issues with white people. They nearly always make less than a full statement of their innermost reactions toward their social problems and personal frustrations. Sometimes under certain conditions of extreme provocation a Negro will make an angry protest. But calm and dependable opinions can be had only when Negroes obtain enough education to permit them to share opinions and to discuss problems with objectivity and a degree of economic security. White southerners on the whole have been more garrulous and emotional, and they have freely revealed their feelings. The Negro on the other hand has been a victim of fear and has most often remained silent. To speak out of turn could mean serious consequences for him, maybe even loss of life.

Failure of free and full communication between whites and Negroes has become a deep social tragedy in the South. Since the days of slavery, the Negro's word against that of a white man has had little or no worth, and, partly because of this, Negroes have feared retributions of various sorts. By long tradition southern whites have generally remained away from Negro assemblies. Once slave and master shared a common communion in churches, but after the Civil War this ceased to be true. It is true that Negroes have stood on the outskirts of political gatherings and listened to political orations. They even gathered on the fringes of the Bilbo audiences to hear him excoriate their race in the bitterest of language. Even so, there has been much to Thomas Nelson Page's contention that close friendships prevailed between southern whites and individual Negroes. Long years of peaceful associations at work and in community relationships document this fact. It is in this area that the present South must rebuild harmonious social relationships. Here is the place where the greatest immediate gains in the future have to be made. Lines of communication must be re-established, and the two races will have to approach their mutual problems with good faith and intellectual honesty. This places upon leadership of both races a rather heavy burden of allaying extremist emotions, of erasing old scars of disharmony, and of making compromises which will actually show that southerners can and will solve their problems democratically and equitably.

Nevertheless the deep underlying fear between the two races must be overcome. Few rural southerners over fifty years of age have not heard in their youth rumors that a race riot was imminent. Country newspapers of half a century ago carried hints of the prevailing anxieties in various communities over this fact. The pro-segregationist literature of the present also contains a tone of fear of the Negro. Possibly no negative fact between the two races is so thoroughly established as the white man's fear of the Negro sexual lust. Based upon strict objective facts of history, the fear should be the other way around, but no clearly defined and dependable notion seems to prevail either privately or in print as to how the Negro man might feel toward the white man's violation of the Negro woman.

It may be that the nearest statement of feeling of Negroes is to be found in a book published by the University of North Carolina Press entitled *What the Negro Wants*. Some of the essays in this book outline more clearly than ever before the Negro's position in regard to this ticklish aspect of southern social relationships. In his *Caste and Class in a Southern Town* John Dollard likewise discusses racial sexual relationships with a high degree of frankness and assurance. Many lynching victims between the years 1880 and 1915 bore placards strung about their necks proclaiming rape as a major cause for lynching. Dependable research, however, has disproved this contention. Murder and assault were the major provoca-

tions, but behind these crimes were the abject fears of the white South of the Negro. This was a fear engendered in the region as early as the Denmark Vesey and Nat Turner rebellions.

Fears of race riots have largely disappeared over the years. When the last of the bitterest of the old political race-baiters like James K. Vardaman, Ben Tillman, and Thomas E. Watson passed on, much of this lurking fear was dissipated. It passed out with the halting of lynching, and with periodic threats of the passage of federal anti-lynching legislation. The explanation of this changing phase of southern social history no doubt lies more closely in the fact that the South is speaking less and less with its frontier voice and has seen great changes in its basic economic structure.

In the present South, the age-old fears are expressed differently. The charge that compliance with the 1954 Supreme Court decision would bring about a commingling and mongrelization of the races has a background in the old fears that resulted in frequent lynchings. Historically large numbers of white men have not been able to trust themselves in the presence of Negro women, and they appear to be certain that intimate and casual relationships in the classroom will rip away the racial barrier. Roy Wilkins, speaking for the NAACP on the television program "Meet the Press" in 1958, answered a question about mongrelization by saying that the presence of so large a number of mulattoes in American society indicates that concern over the mongrelization issue is fully two centuries too late.

If the southern white man has an inborn fear of the Negro, he also has deep suspicion of the intentions of northerners. Just as it has been said that many southerners like the individual Negro and fear the race, it may be said they are fond of the individual northerner and suspect his tribe. Southerners have difficulty in this modern age deciding who the Yankee is. Is he *Life, Time, Look,* and the other slick magazines? Is he nine members of the United States Supreme Court, the NAACP, Adam Clayton Powell, Senator Paul Douglas, Hubert Humphrey, G. Mennen Williams, or Henry and Clare Boothe Luce, or Mrs. Eleanor Roosevelt? Geographically the southerner has difficulty in locating the North. In his mind its centers are New York, Detroit, Chicago, and maybe Los Angeles. But it may be any place where criticism of the South originates. It might even be in Memphis, if such were the case. Possibly there is no physical line, but it is to be located more specifically in terms of emotions, social attitudes, and political reactions. It is the point where often blind prejudices shade off into a doctrinaire certainty of a single solution to the problems of the South.

Everywhere southerners seek to sort out the Yankees: in social gatherings, in business dealings, in politics, and in public discussions. A group of South Carolina high school boys returning from a brief training period at the Great Lakes Training Base asks a Delta Airlines stewardess almost pleadingly whether or not she is a Yankee. It is the eternal triangle of the Negro, the Yankee, and the Southern conscience which causes emotional struggle over the age-old issue of the southern way of life.

The South cannot exist happily, if at all, without the nation, and the nation in turn is dependent upon the South. Somewhere calm and responsible leadership must prevail to solve the larger issues of the race problem. The South can ill afford to continue to waste its emotional energies and further expend its precious resources in the negative approaches used since 1954 without suffering irreparable damages. Extremists on both sides of the issue have yet to offer durable solutions to racial confusions. The solution lies almost solely in the area of the repeated and implied promises that the South can find the answers to its problems. The finding of these answers,

however, places a heavy and positive responsibility upon both social and political leadership to take a careful look at the region's needs and then attempt to bring about solutions in the best of faith and by the sanest possible legislation. The challenge is even greater to everyday citizens, churchmen, newspaper editors, educators, and businessmen. Solutions, however, cannot be accomplished in an atmosphere of bitter denunciation, denial of the law, threatened economic and social boycott and retribution, or dynamitings and other forms of violence.

The negative approach to solving the South's racial issues has the pressure of history against it. On the positive side there is enough calm leadership and dignity in the South to face the current social issues without flinching. It can, of course, by patience and use of good judgment find the answers to all of the region's problems. They will not be simple answers easily arrived at, but they will set the foot of the South on the road to progress.

No one can write a prescription for solving so complex and ancient a problem as that which faces the South at the moment. It seems, however, reasonable to make some general assumptions. Southerners are unaccustomed to gauging the complexity of the race problems—and others as well—on the basis of a full statistical consideration. As a result, they more often than not lose perspective in viewing actual conditions. For instance, it has been the experience of the border areas where schools have been desegregated that Negroes have not flocked to integrated classes in overwhelming numbers. Actually little more than token registrations have occurred. Too, there is a sobering lesson in the fact that these desegregated schools, including Norfolk, Virginia, have been free of unhappy incidents. Where traditionally white universities and colleges have opened their classrooms to Negroes, remarkably small numbers have registered. The more accurate gauge is to be found in the enrollment of Negro colleges, and there is at present no indications that a reduction has or will occur at any time in the foreseeable future. Again, in the political area, the Negro has neither broken nor altered the political behavior pattern of a community where he has exercised his freedom to vote. There has been little if any bloc voting. Sometimes one would conclude from the arguments of the extremists that the Negro has a capacity for leadership and change which the white man does not possess. By the sheer matter of statistics the Negro, except in certain intensely colored areas of the old blackbelt, can hardly alter the political picture in the dire way predicted by the prophets of doom.

The South's economic and social life has been developed around the two races. Both have made major contributions to the region, and a calm and objective evaluation of these contributions offers a key to future peaceful relationships. To attempt to write off or belittle Negro contributions to southern culture would be akin to disowning the contributions of large segments of the white race itself. Here is a broad common ground for the two races to base a positive and mutual respect for the accomplishments of each other.

Many writers stress the distinctiveness of the South of the past and contend that the South of the future will continue to remain different from the mainstream of American life. HARRY S. ASHMORE (b. 1916) disagrees. Recognizing that the South in the half century after the Civil War was different from the remainder of the nation, he has seen the region's distinguishing characteristics vaporizing in the mid-twentieth century. He has therefore written an "epitaph for Dixie." As editor of the *Arkansas Gazette,* Ashmore was awarded a Pulitzer prize for his courageous stand during the 1957 violent desegregation crisis at Little Rock's Central High School. He is presently executive vice president of the Center for the Study of Democratic Institutions at Santa Barbara, California.*

Harry S. Ashmore

The Peculiar Institutions

In the half century after the Civil War the peculiar institution of slavery was reshaped into three institutions of equal peculiarity. Sharecropping was perhaps the only feasible answer for white men, who had land and no cash resources, and for freedmen, who had no land and only agricultural skills. The monolithic structure of one-party politics, which was to give the region disproportionate power in national affairs, was created not for that calculated purpose but as a device for disfranchising the Negro. The "separate but equal" doctrine came into being as a means of keeping the races apart in the schools and other places of public accommodation— serving, certainly, to nurture race prejudice, but accepted, North and South, as a means of preserving order.

These, then, were the institutions—the agrarian economy, the one-party political system, and legal segregation—that gave the region its unique character in the twilight period when it struggled with its internal problems and stubbornly rejected the concepts that prevailed in the republic of which it was a reluctant part. Around them were created the conventions that ordered the Southern society. From them stemmed the slogans that held together a solid bloc of Southern politicians: tariff for revenue only, states rights, and white supremacy. Yet the peculiar institutions were under great pressure from their inception.

As an emergency measure, sharecropping served its purpose; in the long haul it proved as economically unsound as the slavery which had preceded it, creating a landless peasantry which included whites as well as Negroes and provided no stable base for the region's social and economic structure. One-party politics kept the Negro away from the polls, but it did nothing to promote efficiency in government while it did much to improve the fortunes of the demagogues who arose to prey upon the Southern people. The system of legal segregation was marked by inherent injustices which nagged always at the Southern conscience, and in time it became the source of mounting discontent among those who were segregated.

These internal pressures were matched by great forces working from without. As the century turned, a shrinking world began to pull the South back into the mainstream of history. An era of accelerating progress in communications brought the automobile, which made the most remote farm a suburb of the city, and spread newspapers and magazines away from the rail lines. Voices, and then pictures, began coming through the air, and ideas and concepts reached Southerners direct, without first passing through the filter of their own leadership. The Southern people, who had been rooted to the land, became mobile. Two wars sent the young men of the region to far places, and created a vast industrial boom which attracted tides of out-migration toward the centers of economic opportunity. There was a significant in-migration, too, as industry began a countermove to the South to exploit the region's benign climate, untapped natural resources, and vast labor pool.

The peculiar institutions could not escape the profound impact of these physical changes. The gasoline engine which powered the automobile also made possible the new tools of mechanized agriculture, reducing the demand for hand labor which was the basis of the sharecropping system. The steady increase of industrial job opportunities began to lessen the bitter economic competition between Negroes and whites. The fabulous growth of the cities and the corresponding decline of the rural South brought a great expansion of the white-collar middle-class, deeply wounded in the pocketbook by taxes and ready to provide the Republicans a respectable base upon which to erect a second party. The unions followed the factories south, giving indigenous strength to the political Left, which opposes segregation as an article of faith. And the great redistribution of population pulled down the proportion of Negroes to whites to such a degree that the maintenance of legal segregation began to lose its practical urgency over much of the region.

These changes have been accompanied by a marked rise in the status of the Southern Negro. He still remains at the bottom of the social and economic scale, making up a large part of the region's rural and urban slum population, not yet free of the traditional role of drawer of water and hewer of wood. But his physical condition has improved markedly, and his opportunities are slowly but surely broadening. In the cities there is now emerging a Negro middle class—solid, respectable, and conservative—in the void that previously existed between the upper strata of professional workers and the mass of common laborers. If the Negro's usual job is still menial, his pay has risen in geometric progression, and his increased purchasing power has made him a positive factor in the Southern economy.

The most spectacular changes have come in the Negro's legal status, which has been completely redefined in a period of twenty years. He now enjoys, or has the support of the courts in his efforts to obtain, all the guarantees and protections of the United States constitution. And it is a significant mark of his progress that he won most of these rights for himself on the field of legal battle; in earlier campaigns for simple justice he relied upon the leadership of sympathetic Southern whites, but in the series of historic actions in which he regained the franchise and saw the limits of legal segregation progressively narrowed, he fought under his own banner and in his own right.

An age is not born without pangs; an age does not die without giving cause for grief. Southerners have mixed feelings about the vast changes of the mid-century. They like the new prosperity, which for the first time in their memory has produced the pleasant sound of loose change rattling in Southern pockets. But the more sensitive among them flinch at the crassness of the new age. Those with white skin view with varying degrees of alarm the Negro's successful assaults upon the institution of segregation, which have brought him now to the last stronghold of the public schools. Those with dark skin approach the new age with caution—and there is no sign of slackening in the tide of out-migration.

The New South, like the Old, still looks upon the accommodation of the Negro as its greatest single social problem. But the dimensions of the dilemma have changed significantly. The peculiar institutions were erected around the Negro; they set him apart, as they set the region apart, and if they inhibited him in some ways they protected him in others. Flowing from them were a set of conventions accepted by both races and providing the basis for an orderly if uneven social structure. Fundamentally, the relationship was that of master and servant. At its worst it worked great hardships and gross cruelties upon those cast in the lesser role. At its best it embodied the concept of *noblesse oblige* and carried with it the obligation of the strong to sustain the weak. And there was nothing in the institutions, or the conventions, to proscribe warm relationships between individual whites and Negroes.

I have had occasion to reflect upon this in personal terms. As a boy growing up in South Carolina, my experiences were shared with dozens of Negroes—the nurse who tended me until my legs grew long enough to carry me beyond her reach; the cook; the ice man; the grocer's delivery boy; the swarm of Negro children who lived along the dirt streets beyond the white neighborhood; the house servants and the field hands on the cotton farm where I spent the summers. My daughter, growing up in comparable social and economic circumstances in a Southern state, knows only one Negro well enough to call by name—the part-time maid who is regarded as a convenience, not a member of the family. Will she come to know other Negroes as she advances toward maturity? Probably, but not in the same informal way I came to know Mary and Carrie and Nathaniel and Dan and the others who crowd my memory as I write this. Under the Supreme Court's new dispensation it is probable that some Negroes will find their way into the public school she attends, and she is certain to count Negroes among her college classmates. But the schools have changed too; they are no longer durable institutions where a child follows his parents into the same mellowing building to sit at the feet of the same teacher; the mobility of our age has robbed the relationships of the classroom of permanence, and the social orbit no longer revolves around them. Who can remember when he last sat at table with a grammar school classmate? In the connotations of the answer, I suspect, lies the ultimate, practical solution to the immediate problem of integration in public education. But they have not yet provided an answer to the emotional crisis that besets the region.

In the private places of their minds many white Southerners would agree with Albert Dent, the Negro president of Dillard University, who has said that in retrospect they would one day look upon the Supreme Court's segregation decisions as the beginning of their own emancipation—the dawn of the day when they may at last put down the spiritual burden that comes with being on the wrong side of a moral issue. But at the moment the South faces the practical problem of creating a new social order to replace a system already eroded to the point where effective communication between the races no longer exists.

The void is not unique to the South. In the new Negro ghettoes that have mushroomed in all the great industrial centers of the nation, colored people still live apart, behind barriers of extralegal segregation. For the mass the migration of the last generation has been horizontal; only the outstanding few have begun vertical ascent in the social structure. But there is a fundamental difference. The non-South, newly confronted with large concentrations of Negroes, has found their accommodation on terms of full equality a problem, but insists that it can and will be solved; the South so far has simply refused to face it.

So, outwardly, the old tragic pattern repeats itself. In 1958, as in 1860, the region finds itself standing alone in naked defiance of the nation's declared public policy. Now, as then, the border states have fallen away to go with the Union; the roll call of states that voluntarily abandoned segregation in the wake of the 1954 Supreme Court decision has a historic ring: Delaware, Maryland, the District of Columbia, West Virginia, Kentucky, Missouri, and Oklahoma.

Briefly the Upper South wavered, but in the end its leaders bowed to the Deep South. Now Byrd of Virginia marches with Talmadge of Georgia, Fulbright of Arkansas with Eastland of Mississippi; the moderate voices are stilled and the hotspurs are in the saddle. Once again a solid political front extends from the Potomac to the Rio Grande.

But behind the front the South is far from solid. A great deal, of course, depends upon where you are. In the nature of the distribution of population, and the local political situation, a man is likely to be more excited in

Louisiana than in Tennessee, in Alabama than in North Carolina. Out on the fringes the new Southern cause has generated considerable passion; in the rural places the hot-eyed orators once again holler nigger and conjure up their evil visions. But the cold atavistic wind of fear has produced more bewilderment than anger. The prevailing mood is escapist; actuality is not yet at hand, and most Southerners still hope that somehow it will go away.

This time around even those who have mounted the barricades know, and privately concede, that the cause was lost before it was launched; there is no glory here, only bitterness. The battlecry is not "On to victory" but "Not in this generation." This rearguard action has been aptly described by Ralph McGill of the *Atlanta Constitution* as guerrilla fighting among the ruins of the old segregated society; it can be brutal, and it can delay the orderly process of transition, but it cannot turn back the forces that are reshaping the Southern region in the nation's image.

The primary battlegrounds will be in the courts, the legislatures, and the Congress; and a generation of litigation is in prospect. But no people can live forever with an impasse and—sooner in the Upper South than the Deep—the effort will be resumed to find a rational means of adjusting the attitude of the prevailing white majority, which is not yet willing to accept the Negro as an equal, to that of the colored minority, which is no longer willing to accept anything less.

The task, as I have suggested, is complicated by the breakdown of communication between the races—the drawing apart which began when the Negro rejected those social conventions that carry with them a connotation of inferiority. But bridges have been erected, and despite the alarums and excursions of the moment, they still stand and there is traffic across them. At the top level of the educational structure, in the graduate schools of most Southern universities, Negroes and whites have been studying together for almost a decade. On the political front, the emergence of the Negro as a voting citizen has given him new leverage on the machinery of government; Negroes have not yet achieved public office in significant number, but they have found their place in the private places where campaign strategy is plotted. The court decisions have served to give the moral issue of segregation a new focus, and there is great ferment in the churches. The Southern denominations, Protestant and Catholic, including those that split off from their parent bodies in the Civil War, have now taken the occasion to affirm their belief that forced racial segregation is contrary to the Christian ethic.

There are those who profess a willingness to guard the approaches to these bridges with their lives, but they are a comparatively small minority; their support among the rank and file is passive, and it takes more than acquiescence to maintain a crusade. Once there were only two American attitudes toward the Negro: the passionate conviction that he must forthwith be admitted at every level of society as a matter of moral right, and the equally passionate conviction that survival of the white race required that he be barred forever from social intercourse with his masters. Today there is a third attitude: indifference. It may be seen in the Southern generation that fought the Second World War. Few of its members share their fathers' deep emotional concern with the crumbling of the peculiar institutions; if they cannot be aroused to

battle for the rights of the downtrodden blacks, neither are they willing to pay the price of blind opposition to the Negro's effort to gain a higher place in the social scale. The view from the picture window of a suburban ranch house may be no clearer than that framed by the pillars of a porticoed veranda, but it is different—and as the older generation surrenders the places of power this is the view that increasingly will prevail.

So it does not seem to me premature to begin the preparation of an epitaph for Dixie. Will the New South be a better place than the Old? Materially, almost certainly. Spiritually, perhaps. Behind the façade of harsh words and extremist laws there is already emerging the pattern in which the South will finally accommodate its dwindling Negro population as it moves from second- to first-class citizenship; it will be imperfect but reasonably effective, and in the end it will be far easier to achieve than the accommodation produced by trial and error in the bloodshot aftermath of Reconstruction. But the transition can be accomplished only at the expense of the qualities that made the South distinctive, and cast it in the remarkable role it has played in the history of the Republic. Perhaps, a generation from now when the last shovelful of earth is patted down on the grave, we shall be able to see the vanishing age more clearly, to examine its virtues without being distracted by its faults. There will be, I think, other than sentimental reasons for mourning its passing.

Each of the preceding authors dwelt on the Negro as a crucial factor in the distinctive South. In contrast, the next four selections focus on the top of the Southern social scale in the search for the South's identity. The writers point out that the aristocrats of the South—and the attitudes of all southerners toward them—have greatly affected the course of Southern history. The first selection is by LOUIS B. WRIGHT (b. 1889), who limits his remarks to the development of an aristocracy in colonial Virginia modeled after the English gentry, but his essay has implications for the entire South and nation. A native of South Carolina, Wright was from 1942 to 1968 Director of the Folger Shakespeare Library, Washington, D.C. He is author of *The Atlantic Frontier* (1947), *Culture on the Moving Frontier* (1955), and *The Cultural Life of the American Colonies, 1607–1763* (1957).*

Louis B. Wright

Development of
a Virginia Aristocracy

Virginia has never hid her light under a bushel, nor let others forget the contributions of her sons to the development of the social, political, and intellectual life of the nation. And Virginia's pride in her past is well justified. Particularly in statecraft, in the early periods of our history, Virginia was surpassed by no other region in the number of leaders possessed of good breeding, intelligence, and wisdom. Even yet the tradition of a cultured and intelligent leadership has not completely disappeared from the political life of that commonwealth, for the tradition is fortunately tenacious, and ancient as such things go in America. Virginia, moreover, in

the seventeenth and early eighteenth centuries developed a way of life and a certain aristocratic outlook which, if not always acceptable to other localities, nevertheless profoundly influenced the course of American history. . . .

The tight little aristocracy that developed in Virginia in the later years of the seventeenth century quickly gained a power and influence far in excess of the numerical importance of its members, who were vastly outnumbered by the yeoman class. Planter-aristocrats ruled Virginia as by prescriptive right, and from the ranks of their descendants came statesmen who helped weld thirteen

*Louis B. Wright, *The First Gentlemen of Virginia: Intellectual Qualities of the Early Colonial Ruling Class* (San Marino, Calif., 1940), pp. 1–4, 38–39, 45–46, 48–50, 53–55, 59–62. Reprinted without footnotes by permission of the author and the Henry E. Huntington Library and Art Gallery.

rebellious colonies into a nation. The mental qualities of Virginia's Revolutionary leaders depended upon something more than the mere demand of a great emergency. Back of them lay a tradition of training for leadership—the tradition of the country gentleman who had learned to assume as his natural obligation certain political and social responsibilities. . . .

Many books and a still greater number of earnest essays have been written by loyal Virginians in a pious effort to make manifest their descent from noble or aristocratic English houses. Occasionally, having fallen short of credible fact, these efforts have prompted satirical comment from unsympathetic readers who find it hard to believe that so many descendants of Edward III—and even of William the Conqueror—should have found their way to a single colony in the New World. One historian, callously surveying the lists of emigrants in the seventeenth and eighteenth centuries, sardonically suggests that the archives of Newgate Prison and the Old Bailey might prove a more fruitful source of genealogical information than the records of the peerage. The truth, however, is in neither extreme. No one well informed in colonial history is so naïve as to maintain that Virginia was won from the forest and the Indian by aristocratic settlers in silken doublets. Nor can the view be substantiated that jailbirds and the scum of English port towns played any important part in the colonial settlement. As was the case in most of the other colonies, the majority of the Virginia settlers were hard-working folk bent upon bettering their economic lot. Though Virginia probably attracted more emigrants of gentle birth than any of the other North American colonies, unimpeachable proof of important social connections in England cannot be found for most of the so-called First Families. The significant fact is not the social position of their ancestors, but what they became in a world of their own making. . . .

Despite realistic facts produced by a generation of hard-working historians, an imaginary concept of colonial Virginia has taken shape in popular belief. In this fanciful picture—a picture frequently drawn in nineteenth-century fiction—rich and romantic Cavaliers lived in feudal splendor, surrounded by multitudes of retainers. Great houses, filled with furniture and finery brought from England, provided a background for these barons of the Virginia rivers. There the lords and ladies of the new dispensation spent their leisure in cultivating the social graces. With dancing, gaiety, and decorous flirtation they passed the time in Arcadia. . Only dueling disturbed the idyllic dream, for in Arcadia gentlemen were touchy about their honor and a duel at dawn under the oaks beside a dark river was the invariable method of settling personal disputes—in the novels that described the dream world of early Virginia. These silken-coated grandees were all descended from some ancient and distinguished family of England—preferably from some knight who came over with William the Conqueror—and titles in the family trees of the colonists were thicker than dogwood blooms in spring. Thus have romancers imagined Virginia in colonial days, and so firmly has the idea become established that some patriotic antiquarians have struggled vainly to prove its truth. Contributors to the genealogical magazines of the South too often have had an obsession concerning the nobility of their ancestors.

Romantically absurd as some of the notions of colonial Virginia have been, there is nevertheless a germ of truth in the imaginary picture of life there. Virginia did develop an aristocracy of wealthy planters, who, in time, came to live in considerable splendor, who established a pattern of life modeled after the English gentry, who ruled the destinies of the colony as by inherited right. Even though this development was gradual, and the more magnificent manifestations of this aristocracy came late in the colonial period, the seventeenth century saw the evolution of a hierarchic social order with a few great planters at the top. If realistic historians, revolting at the nonsense of many genealogical claims, have been moved to emphasize the essentially plebeian quality of the vast majority of Virginia settlers, we must not forget that the men who ruled the colony from its inception made up an aristocracy whose power and influence were out of all proportion to their numbers. If the majority of Virginia colonists were simple, hard-working folk of no ancestral pretensions and little wealth, the families who controlled them and their destinies soon became both wealthy and proud. It is not necessary to assume, however, that even these members of the ruling class were aristocratic in their origins. A few were, most were not. But, having reached Virginia and become possessed of great tracts of land which assured them wealth, power, and social recognition, they quickly assumed all the prerogatives of the aristocratic order they had known in England. Though latter-day worshipers of democracy may discern the seeds of popular government in colonial Virginia, actually the government, from the first settlement to the Revolution, was aristocratic, even oligarchic. . . .

The introduction of the African slave system was the most important single factor in the evolution of the Virginia aristocracy, for it enabled wealthy planters to crush, perhaps unconsciously, the economic power of small landowners who depended upon their own labor. Wealthy men, able to take up increasing acreages of new land and farm them profitably with slaves, succeeded where poor men, confined to lesser holdings, soon exhausted their farms by overcultivation of tobacco, and either had to face failure or push on into frontier regions. The influence of slavery upon the social structure of colonial Virginia was far-reaching, extending even to subtle changes in manners and behavior. . . .

Its immediate effect was to make possible an aristocracy of rich planters who in time learned to value the amenities of a genteel life.

During the period of settlement, . . . the fundamental fact determining social status was capital. That some families were founded by the sons of gentlemen was of far less importance at the moment than whether they had money enough to bring over servants and take up large tracts of land. The tradesman, the merchant, and the gentleman who were adequately financed at the start gained a similar foothold in the economic structure of the colony, and, if they prospered sufficiently, they all became members of the ruling class, and, in the course of time, developed similar ideas about family, position, and social obligations. All of them had definite notions of what they would do with wealth, once they had attained it: they would become landed proprietors as much as possible like the country gentry of England, but they would adapt their "gentility" to the requirements of new conditions. And, whatever their background, that is what they did. . . .

The economic development of Virginia made for the division of society into three main groups: servants and slaves, yeomanry, and a ruling class of great planters. During the first fifty years conditions were most favorable to white servants' graduating into yeomen—that is to say, into small independent farmers who worked their tobacco plots with only such aid as their families could give them. A few of these yeomen—fewer than one might suppose—rose to positions of some consequence as members of the House of Burgesses or as holders of county offices; but, from the later years of the seventeenth century, as large plantations multiplied and great planters became more powerful, the yeomen had less and less political or social importance.

Virginia's preoccupation with tobacco culture to the exclusion of other sources of wealth discouraged the growth of towns until very late in the colonial period and prevented the development of a commercial middle class like that of New England. In Virginia, the one goal of every settler was to get land and raise tobacco. Since tobacco exhausted the soil in a few years, fresh land was constantly needed; hence, for successful farming, larger tracts were required than was the case in New England, where farmers lived close together in compact villages and usually shared common wood lots and pasture land. In Virginia, on the contrary, there was no incentive, even among small farmers, to live together in villages, and the size of the larger plantations made for scattered homesteads, each more or less economically independent of the others. Since the great planters, with shipping connections in England, imported all the commodities needed for themselves and their less opulent neighbors, and had the goods delivered directly to their wharves along the rivers, there was little opportunity for the development of a class of middlemen—importers, merchants, shopkeepers, bankers—the people who normally make up the population of trading centers. London and Bristol were the trading towns of Virginia planters. In the early days, even craftsmen were exceedingly scarce. Carpenters, blacksmiths, weavers, shoemakers, and other artisans who managed to reach Virginia, more often than not abandoned their trades to become growers of the profitable Indian weed. Instead of settling in villages and developing industries as they did in New England, they, too, scattered up and down the rivers as small farmers. With no organized independent middle class to check the power of the wealthier planters and with a yeomanry that became steadily weaker and less assertive as slave competition increased, the growth of a dominant aristocracy was inevitable.

By the mid-seventeenth century, the progress of the wealthier planters toward the prosperity and power that became so marked a few generations later had already begun. If not many planters at this time had much to boast about in the way of houses and furnishings, at least a few were already well established, with comfortable homes. . . .

From the first, the control of most governmental offices was in the hands of men of rank and position. If a few yeomen by superior ability and unusual industry managed to obtain offices, the vast majority of political posts were filled by the higher order of planters. . . .

At the top of the hierarchy of government officials were the members of the Council of State, generally called simply "the Council"—a small body of the highest-ranking men in the colony. Their power was so great and their offices and duties so multifarious that a recital of them sounds like a burlesque of government in a Gilbert and Sullivan opera. They constituted the Upper House in the Assembly, corresponding to the House of Lords in England; they sat as a General Court to hear the most serious criminal and civil cases in the colony; as members of the Council, they were exempt from arrest and from certain levies; and they had many individual offices and duties. . . . Virginia had no titled aristocracy, but it had an equivalent in the great ones who sat in the Council of State.

By the later years of the seventeenth century, the evolution of a Virginia aristocracy had progressed to a point where a small ruling class not only monopolized public offices but also, by that very fact, dominated the economic life of the colony. Officeholders, from members of the Council down to the lesser officials of the counties, were often able to use their posts for personal profit. Nor does this mean that they were necessarily dishonest. Legitimate emoluments and perquisites of office, such as fees received by collectors of customs, helped to enrich officials. Occasionally, however, great men added to their possessions by highhanded, if not culpable, methods. For example, Edward

Hill, the lord of Shirley, was charged in 1677 with appropriating public property to his own use but claimed that the charges were made by malicious persons, spiteful because of his part in suppressing the Bacon rebellion. With the haughtiness of a Coriolanus, Hill, in a lengthy defense, expresses the aristocrat's contempt of "that hydra the vulgar"—the ignorant "rout of people" who clamor against him. He may have had too little of the sense of public responsibility that went with the gentleman's position, but at least he had the pride of place which became such a notable characteristic of the Virginia aristocracy.

By the end of the seventeenth century, the aristocracy was supreme. Headed by the members of the Council, the ruling class monopolized land to such an extent that immigrants had difficulty finding homesteads, and poor farmers in need of fresh land had to migrate to the frontier. . . .

The members of this upper class were eternally conscious of their superiority, and were diligent to see that the lower orders of society observed distinctions in rank. As early as 1674, evidence of social stratification is provided by the case of a tailor, James Bullock, resident of York County, who scandalized the gentlemen of that district by presuming to enter his mare against a horse owned by Dr. Matthew Slader in a race for a purse of two thousand pounds of tobacco. For such presumption, the tailor was fined one hundred pounds of tobacco by the justices, who declared that racing was "a sport for gentlemen only." Deference was demanded and generally received as a right by the upper classes; when some rude yokel failed in the respect he was supposed to show to superiors, he might be fined. More serious than contempt of court was the offense of William Hatton when, in 1662, he declared that the justices of the peace of York County were a lot of "coopers, hog-trough makers, peddlers, cobblers, tailors, weavers, and not fitting to sit where they do sit." Because he had reflected upon the social status of the gentlemen of the county, he was made to eat his words. Gentlemen were quick to invoke the law against common fellows who so far forgot themselves as to be impudent toward their betters.

Having acquired the estate and dignity of country gentlemen, Virginia planters soon began to yearn for coats of arms—for recognition from the College of Heralds of their ancient lineages. The eagerness of the Virginia gentry for coat armor is significant of their desire to be of the gentry, to be like the aristocracy in the mother country. . . . The ruling class . . . nearly all managed to lay claim to coat armor. According to one Virginia antiquarian, over one hundred and fifty colonial families had a "vested right" to it. Although such a statement would be hard to substantiate, the truth is that, by the beginning of the eighteenth century, nearly every family of any social pretension could boast a copy of its coat of arms. Prosperous planters wanted not only the position and prestige of the ancient gentry but also the visible tokens of this much-desired state.

By the first quarter of the eighteenth century, there were enough families of aristocratic standing to make something of a show in the "society" of the little capital of Williamsburg . . . [and] the evolution of the Virginia gentry had reached its first stage of maturity. The lines of social stratification that were to persist for generations were now plainly marked. A few great families that in future years were to influence the destiny of the whole country had already risen to power. Traditional attitudes toward the various social groups had had time to become established. Virginia had developed the social characteristics that largely shaped its history for the next century.

Harvard-trained CLEMENT EATON (b. 1898), a native of North Carolina, spent most of his professional years, until his retirement in 1968, explaining the essence of the Old South to graduate students at the University of Kentucky. Among his many volumes dealing with that region are: *Freedom of Thought in the Old South* (1940), *A History of the Southern Confederacy* (1954), and *The Mind of the Old South* (1964). Eaton agrees with Wright that the colonial society of the South was dominated by an aristocracy, and he points out in this selection that when the descendants of these coastal aristocrats migrated westward, in the early nineteenth century, they carried with them the country gentleman ideal.*

Clement Eaton

The Country Gentleman Ideal

Charleston was a unique Southern city, where an unusual blend of planters and gentleman merchants formed the upper class, as the Reverend Abiel Abbott of Beverly, Massachusetts, found in 1818. Among the cultivated people he met was the son of Ralph Izard, one of the grandees of the rice country, who took him to his estate, the Elms, seventeen miles from the city, and showed him the kind of life led by affluent country gentlemen.

The plantation mansion was a spacious building in the Adam style, erected in 1809. Abbott was pleased with the "perfect servants" who brushed his clothes and polished his shoes, and with the Carolina breakfast of tea, coffee, johnnycake, grits, and eggs. The mildness of the task system of slavery, which allowed the slave one-third to one-half of the day for leisure, surprised him. The daughter of the family entertained him with a concert on the harp and the master conversed at tea "with much knowledge of the world and books." The Izards were representative of the Carolina country gentry, a well-knit ruling class, whose power and prestige had been diminished by the Revolution but who nevertheless retained great vitality even after the rise of Jacksonian democracy in the 1820's.

A potent force in the development of plantation society was the ideal of the English country gentleman. Although there were country squires in other parts of the United States, notably in the Hudson Valley and

*From pp. 1–8, *The Growth of Southern Civilization, 1790–1860* by Clement Eaton. Copyright © 1961 by Clement Eaton. Reprinted by permission of Harper & Row, Publishers. Footnotes omitted.

around Narragansett Bay, they did not fix the tone of society or dominate the social pattern as those in the Southern tidewater did. The majority of planters did not know at first hand how English squires lived, but the tradition had been handed down from the colonial period and strengthened by the reading of English and Scottish novels. This institution had been modified greatly by the Southern environment, particularly by the discarding of its tenantry basis and the exaggeration of certain aspects of the English model, such as carrying the defense of personal honor to ridiculous extremes. The growth of large plantations and of Negro slavery in the eighteenth century immeasurably strengthened the position of the country gentry in the South. Other forces which tended to perpetuate the old English institution here were the vestry system of the Church of England; the county court, with its justices of the peace; the sway of family in local government; and, to some degree, the illusion of cavalier origins. These influences counteracted the leveling effect of the American frontier.

The ideal of the country gentleman was carried by emigrating Virginians and Carolinians to remote corners of the South. At the close of the ante-bellum period Henry Stanley, the future explorer of Africa, encountered this powerful social force while clerking in a country store in Arkansas. In Cypress Bend he was amazed to see his fellow clerks and the plain farmers who visited the store bowing to a stern code of conduct that was aristocratic in origin—the obligation to uphold personal honor. Even the proprietor of the store, a German Jew, quickly resented any suggestion of insult and used a dueling pistol. And Stanley too, who had spent his childhood in a workhouse in Wales and had been cuffed about as a sailor on a merchant ship, succumbed to the pervasive mores of this Southern community. When he was sent a package containing a chemise and a petticoat because he was tardy in volunteering for the Confederate army, he immediately enrolled in the company of the Dixie Greys.

Pondering the reasons for "the proud sensitive spirit prevailing in Arkansas," Stanley concluded that it was the fruit of a unique type of provincialism nourished on the plantations and lonely homesteads. The touchiness of the people, he thought, was accentuated by the fevers and chills of chronic malaria that affected so many of them. "In New Orleans," he observed, ". . . the social rule was to give and take, to assert an opinion, and hear it contradicted without resort to lethal weapons, but, in Arkansas, to refute a statement was tantamount to giving the lie direct, and was likely to be followed by an instant appeal to the revolver or bowie."

The farther Southern civilization extended from the seacoast, the more diluted were European traditions, but in the tidewater traces of English institutions survived strongly. In the country-gentleman ideal, in the use of British nomenclature in the currency, in government and religion, and in retaining old English pronunciations and even outmoded vestiges of English court practices, such as benefit of clergy, the South of the early republic revealed its affinity for the mother country. Riding through Maryland and the Northern Neck of Virginia in 1796, the Irish traveler Isaac Weld observed that the great plantation residences were "exactly similar to the old manor houses in England." The occupants of these houses lived in "a style, which approaches nearer to that of the English country gentleman than what is to be met [with] anywhere else on the continent. . . ."

In the same year, the architect Benjamin H. Latrobe, freshly arrived from England, noted a striking likeness between the rural society of Virginia and that of his native Yorkshire. So congenial did he find the company of Virginia planters that he remarked, "In Amelia [County] I could have again fancied myself in a society of English country gentlemen . . . had not the shabbiness of their mansions undeceived me." At Petersburg he attended a horse race which he described as "a duodecimo edition of the Newmarket race in folio." Some years later, in 1819, Adam Hodgson, an English traveler, reported that the best society of Charleston was "much superior to any which I have yet seen in America." The manners of the upper class resembled those of "the more polished of our country gentlemen and are formed on the model of what in England we call 'the old school.' "

Yet the Southern planters did not keep up their estates as the English squires did. In contrast to the green and neatly tilled farms of England, the countryside of Maryland and Virginia had an unkempt and worn-out aspect, for much of the arable land had been exhausted by unremitting tobacco culture and ruined by erosion. The dilapidated mansions behind stately groves of trees, the abandoned tobacco fields covered by yellow sedge and old field pines, the deserted log cabins, the decay of the Episcopal churches, whose broken-out windowpanes and sagging doors permitted the invasion of pigs and cattle, indicated a serious lack of prosperity and a profound apathy of spirit. Planters and small farmers alike were forced to be largely self-sufficient, making for themselves such domestic articles as cloth, shoes, soap, candles, and furniture. The decline of the tobacco trade after the Revolution had reduced contacts with the great world of Europe. Indeed, before the coming of steamboats and railroads, the farmers and planters of the early republic were isolated both from Europe and the Northern states and were less cosmopolitan in outlook than their fathers and grandfathers had been.

The planters of the tidewater region were reluctant to recognize the realities of a changing economy. Although their plantations might be run down and their Negroes miserably clad, they maintained an uncon-querable pride and refused to alter their ways. Virginians, especially, continued to practice the lavish hospitality of former days. At the close of the eighteenth century, nearly every plantation was overstocked with slaves. Instead of working industriously to improve conditions, many of the planters, according to Weld, "give themselves but little trouble about the management of their plantations." Relying on overseers, they spent many hours hunting and fishing, drinking alcoholic liquors, and simply "doing nothing." Travelers found the inflated manner of speaking of these run-down aristocrats ridiculous, and they were amused by the titles that Southerners profusely conferred on plain citizens. Frequently a stage driver would be addressed as "Captain," an innkeeper as "Colonel," a lawyer or a large planter as "Honorable" or "General."

The economic distress of the old tobacco country was owing partly to the unreliability of the foreign markets upon which it depended. The decline in the tobacco trade to England after the Revolution turned many of the planters of the tidewater area to raising wheat. In the newer lands of the Piedmont, on the other hand, tobacco culture expanded and became the money crop. The Napoleonic wars opened a good, though fluctuating, market for cereals in Europe and the West Indies. When prices of tobacco rose temporarily, the planters abandoned wheat for their old crop. As a consequence, between 1818 and 1822, European markets became glutted with tobacco. When tobacco prices declined, the planters returned to wheat, but the ravages of the Hessian fly and of rust drove them once again to tobacco—"the old hopeless shifting from one crop to another began again." Jefferson gave up tobacco as a money crop at Monticello after 1812, but he continued to cultivate "the royal weed" as the principal crop of Poplar Forest, his plantation in southwestern Virginia.

The towns and ports of the tobacco country reflected the languishing state of agriculture. Particularly noticeable was the decline of Georgetown, Alexandria, Tappahannock, Yorktown, and Norfolk, ports at which great quantities of tobacco had formerly been inspected and exported. By 1800, since little tobacco was now grown in the tidewater, Yorktown had dwindled to a third of its size before the Revolution. Norfolk, the largest commercial town in Virginia, contained only four hundred houses, its unpaved streets were filthy, and it lacked a single bank. Williamsburg, once the center of government and fashion, had so rapidly declined after the removal of the capital to Richmond in 1779 that it was a shadow of its former self. When Benjamin Latrobe walked down its principal street seventeen years later, he noticed that the wooden columns of the capitol were stripped of their moldings and all awry, and many of the houses were ruined and uninhabited. William and Mary College had only thirty students; Jefferson's alma mater had become little more than a grammar school where the boys went barefooted. The fine old Episcopal church of Bruton Parish nearby was neglected and out of repair.

The richest and most flourishing parts of the South at the end of the eighteenth century were the rice and sea-island-cotton districts of the Carolinas and Georgia. Unlike the tobacco lands, the rice fields did not suffer seriously from erosion or the depletion of the soil. The rice district was a narrow strip of swampy land less than fifty miles wide; its extent was determined by the limits within which the tidal ebb and flow of the freshwater rivers and streams could be used to flood and drain the fields. On sea islands that fringed the coast long-staple cotton was very profitably grown. The cultivation of indigo, a crop of the higher lands of the interior, had largely been abandoned as a result of Oriental competition and the loss of the British bounty

after the Revolution. In its place planters had turned, after the invention of the cotton gin, to growing short-staple cotton. In sharp contrast to Virginia, Maryland, and North Carolina, South Carolina enjoyed a period of prosperity and vigorous growth until the panic year of 1819. The exports of sea-island cotton increased enormously, and the cultivation of short-staple cotton expanded rapidly into the Piedmont. Yet within a generation the upland cotton planter had skimmed the cream of fertility from the soil and the eastern part of the state was showing marked decay.

The only considerable urban centers in the Southern states at the opening of the nineteenth century were the seaports of Baltimore and Charleston. Baltimore had a population of 26,111 people, slightly larger than that of Boston, and Charleston contained 20,473 whites and slaves. In both of these cities the merchants held high place in society. In Charleston, where they closed their businesses at four o'clock in the afternoon, they were fond of giving elaborate dinners and entertainments. Of this city President Washington wrote during his Southern journey of 1791: "The inhabitants are wealthy — Gay — and hospitable." The Carolina ladies of the upper class, observed Mrs. Nathanael Greene, widow of the Rhode Island Revolutionary general, who had been given a plantation by the grateful state of Georgia, spent half of their time making their toilets, one-fourth of the remaining time paying and receiving social visits, and another fourth in scolding and hitting the servants. Not all the Carolina ladies, however, lived this vapid existence, for there were some like Eliza Lucas, the introducer of indigo planting into South Carolina, who were active in managing the domestic affairs of the plantation.

Just as the country gentry of England maintained town houses in London, the

Carolina planters lived in Charleston for a large part of the year. Fear of malaria caused many of them every summer to flee from their swampy and mosquito-ridden plantations to the more salubrious atmosphere of Charleston and Sullivan's Island, though many remained on their rice estates, sleeping at night in the pinelands. Their long sojourns in the city made these tidewater planters not only more sophisticated but also more closely-knit in their views. They went to Charleston because of their dread of fever and ague, but also because of their love of the fashionable life there; they all made sure of being in the city during race week in February.

The society of this opulent city practiced what Thorstein Veblen would have called conspicuous leisure, consumption, and display. The Duc de la Rochefoucauld, who traveled in the Southern states in 1795–97, noted that a Charleston gentleman seldom had less than twenty servants in his domestic establishment and that the children had Negro maids and body servants to wait upon them. Abiel Abbott commented, some years later, "No coach moves in Charleston without a negro behind and a negro before." He also observed that house slaves were so numerous that "the Charlestonians are obliged to exercise their wits to devise sufficient variety to keep them employed." Besides enjoying jockey clubs, eating clubs, card playing, and formal balls, some of the upper class organized golf clubs at Savannah and Augusta as early as 1800.

Although South Carolina lacked free schools and relatively few of its planters were masters of Greek and Latin, its capital city displayed such evidences of culture as the St. Cecilia concerts and balls, the Charleston Library Society, founded in 1748, good bookshops, and a small group of amateur naturalists and scientists. The Reverend Mr. Abbott attended dinners given by gentlemen of the city at which the conversation was cultivated and witty, although the guests used "expressions not quite pleasant to the ears of a minister or a lady." He visited the spinster daughters of Dr. David Ramsay, the noted historian, who three years earlier had been murdered on the streets of Charleston by an insane person. In their conversation with him these spinster ladies observed great formality, which he attributed partly to their consciousness of ancestry and partly to their occupation as schoolteachers. The homes of some of the planters, such as Middleton House and Drayton Hall, reminded the Duc de la Rochefoucauld of the residences of ancient English country estates. The Carolina rice planters continued until the Civil War to be more affluent and to live with more style than the tobacco planters of the Chesapeake Bay country.

Accepting the presence and influence of a Southern aristocracy, ROLLIN G. OSTERWEIS (b. 1907) directs his remarks to the "cult of chivalry" which these southerners developed. He argues that this emphasis on chivalry ranks along with slavery and the plantation economy as the chief distinctive features of the region. A Yale University administrator, Osterweis has written *Three Centuries of New Haven, 1638–1938* (1953) and *Charter Number Two: The Centennial History of the First New Haven National Bank* (1963).*

Rollin G. Osterweis

The Cult of Chivalry

The European romantic movement was a literary and artistic effort to create a new set of values, made necessary by the intellectual, social, and political revolutions of the eighteenth century. Romanticism, as a state of mind, had manifested itself in ancient times and in the Renaissance. It became a surging, self-conscious movement during a period of about a hundred years between the approximate dates 1760 and 1860. Basically, it was a revolt of *sensibility* and *imagination* against a preceding age of *form, symmetry, precision, balance,* and *reason.* The essence of the romantic mood was *diversitarianism,* as contrasted with the earlier emphasis on *uniformitarianism.* For the romantic, "One thing alone is needful: Everything." . . .

The romanticisms that evolved in the various European countries resulted from the blending of native conditions, including somewhat spontaneous romantic stirrings, on the one hand, and imported ideas, on the other. A similar development characterized the romantic movement in America—so far as the non-Southern sections of the country were concerned. In England, Scotland, and Ireland, in France, Germany, and Italy—and in the United States north of the Mason and Dixon line—a vast variety of romantic notions characterized the impact. The essence of the mood was indeed diversitarianism.

For the most part the themes associated with European romanticism, sweeping into the American North between the War of 1812

*Rollin G. Osterweis, *Romanticism and Nationalism in the Old South* (New Haven, Conn.: Yale University Press, 1949), pp. 8–11, 16–17, 20–21, 56–57, 213–16. Reprinted by permission of the Yale University Press, Footnotes omitted.

and the war of 1861, found no resistance. Characteristically, they adapted to local environmental features and emerged as the notions of general American romanticism. They are evident in the works of Longfellow, Cooper, and Irving, of Emerson, Melville, and Hawthorne, of Thoreau, Whitman, and Bancroft, of the Hudson River school of painters, of the Greek revival and Gothic revival architects. They are reflected in the humanitarian movements of New England and the religious revival meetings of the Western frontier.

But the effect on the South was vastly different—and Southern romanticism evolved as a complex of themes differentiated from general American romanticism. Southern romanticism, also the product of native factors and imported ideas, was a distinctive and influential force. It helped to create a nation within a nation by 1860. . . .

The essential quality of the romantic mood was diversitarianism and dynamic flux. In most of the areas where it exerted influence during the nineteenth century, there was a restless, variegated affinity for all of its implications but an affinity, in each instance, colored by local considerations. Those considerations gave a certain selectivity to the process of accepting imported notions. For example, the excessive emotional trends, associated with German romanticism, lost intensity in contact with the Cartesian heritage as they made their way into French thought. New England, in the person of Emerson, welcomed the philosophy of Coleridge and rejected the atheism of Shelley.

Despite this evidence of some selectivity in the areas to which romanticism came, the movement generally swept in, accompanied by all its diverse implications. Selective processes followed later. Rejection of a theme or idea came after some acquaintance with it.

This was true throughout Europe and in all of America, except the South. New England read Scott and Dickens, Byron and Coleridge, Schiller and Kant. New Englanders were curious about the social romanticism of Saint-Simon and Fourier. During the pre-Civil War years, Massachusetts was bursting with ideas of romantic philosophy, romantic reform movements, romantic literary independence, romantic historiography, romantic religion. Little wonder that the Bay State produced Emerson, Melville, James Russell Lowell, Dorothea Dix, Bancroft, and Theodore Parker.

But in the South the conditions receptive to romantic themes were different. Between 1815 and 1861, certainly after 1831, the South was a more nearly static society, walled off by a dike that was intended to preserve this static character. Under such circumstances, the romantic movement could not hit the South head on. Rather, the Southerners would determine just which romantic offerings would be permitted to pass through their intellectual blockade. They would choose the particular ideas which they were willing to have circulate. European romanticisms had to pause at the gate of the Southern redoubt for customs inspection. New England's romantic themes, with their emphasis on social reform, were suspect before they ever reached the Dixie border.

Southern romanticism, then, did not exemplify the diversitarian quality identified with the mood in the American North and in Europe. Rather it reflected the presence of a decisive local selectivity. . . .

Behind the Southern social structure of the period lay a complex of traditions, which, viewed as a whole, gave that structure a feudal character. Such structure offered an inevitable receptivity for chivalric notions.

There was the tradition of the Virginia gentleman, a hardy perennial cultivated in the Old Dominion during the eighteenth century. It grew out of a conscious effort to reproduce the patterns of English rural life in the New World and especially to reproduce the country gentleman ideal. There was also the memory of feudal traits associated with the planting of the colonies in Maryland, Virginia, and the Carolinas. The proprietary colony of the Calverts commenced existence with all the trappings of medieval feudalism; Virginia and the Carolinas had an easy familiarity with primogeniture, entail, and quitrents, which contrasted sharply with life in New England. . . .

The plantation of the pre-Civil War South was the counterpart of the medieval manor. The planter was the repository of social dignity, of judicial power, of political leadership, for his neighborhood, in quite the same fashion as the eighteenth-century English squire whom he strove to emulate. Both were survivals of the feudal tradition. The presence of the Negro slaves, however, gave an added intensity to feudal feeling in the South. Here was a factor far closer to the serf of the Middle Ages than anything in Georgian England. Slavery not only heightened class-consciousness among the aristocratic planters but provided a permanent cellar to the social structure, which made the small farmers more satisfied with their lot. The interplay of slavery and feudalism had much to do with shaping this social structure. . . .

Slavery contributed directly to the Southern taste for romantic notions. It freed the dominant planter class from time-consuming drudgery and gave it opportunity to read romantic literature and indulge romantic fancies. It sponsored an exaggerated pride in the ruling group, together with an instinctive habit of command from early childhood. Since it answered the labor problem, both economically and socially, it precluded any concern with social problems such as that displayed in the North. All this fed the affinity for the chivalric theme in romanticism. . . .

That there existed a natural affinity in all this for the theme of medieval chivalry, emphasized by Scott's brand of romanticism, is perfectly obvious. The Southern planter

stood at the top of a stratified society, cherishing the country-gentleman ideal—his lordly sense of leadership fed by the presence of slaves. His code demanded courtesy, deference to women, hospitality to strangers, defense of his honor, consideration for social inferiors. No wonder that he seized upon the *Waverley Novels* with enthusiasm. They convinced him that the chivalric ideal was still to be found, in the very middle of the industrial grime and turmoil of the nineteenth century—to be found in the American South. As for the epitome of that ideal he was, of course, the knightly planter. Wilfred Ivanhoe spelled romantic glamour. A country gentleman should strive to be a chivalrous knight. . . .

During the antebellum period, the Southern gentry, under the romantic impact, flowered by 1850 into the *Southern chivalry;* the name of the cult, by courtesy of Sir Walter's usage, was also employed to describe its votaries. During those same years, the Northern business leaders developed into the *solid citizenry.*

While the dominant class of the North cherished "respectability," that of the South nurtured its "chivalric ideal." To the critical Northerner, the Southern ideal rested on the foul institution of Negro slavery. To the critical Southerner, the civilization above the line was a crude commercialism. By the middle of the century, the land of the "solid citizen" and the land of the "romantic knight" sheltered two separate and distinct civilizations. A clash between them became a serious possibility. The problems relating to slavery and expansion, which grew out of the territorial acquisitions of the Mexican war, reached a crisis during the debates on the Omnibus Bill in 1850. A temporary settlement emerged; but farseeing men realized that it was only temporary. Southern leaders, especially the hardheaded Carolinians like Langdon Cheves, began to seek formulas for a permanent solution.

The transition from the concept of "two distinct civilizations" to the concept of "a nation within a nation" was an easy one. Such a transition was common in Europe all through this period. Romantic nationalism was a cultural nationalism, marked by the striving of repressed cultural groups for expression and for statehood. This was the nationalism of Herder and Michelet—the nationalism which Heine saw implicit in the writings of Walter Scott. It appeared in the painting of Delacroix; and still more in the musical compositions of Chopin and Liszt.

The idea of Southern nationalism, which developed especially in South Carolina during the decade before the Civil War, proved to be the most ambitious notion related to the growth of Southern romanticism. The cult of chivalry characterized the mood in the South more than any other single romantic manifestation and supplied the chief intellectual ingredient for the concept of a differentiated civilization. The idea of Southern nationalism followed as the next logical step.

Through the years between 1815 and 1861, the romantic movement played its role in shaping the course of Southern civilization. . . .

The civilization of the Old South rested on a tripod. Two of the legs—cotton and the plantation system, and the institution of Negro slavery—have been thoroughly analyzed in the past. The third leg, usually designated by the word "chivalry," has been neglected.

Inquiry into the nature of "the third leg" leads into the maze of romanticism; for the cult of chivalry is clearly a manifestation of the romantic movement. And no understanding of Southern romanticism is possible without basic concern for the movement as a whole.

Romantic notions, brought in from Europe and the North, blended with local environmental features to produce the various patterns of Southern romanticism. The fundamental order linking the themes of Southern romanticism derives from a recognition that there were four distinct sets of manifestations identified with four cultural subdivisions.

In the area of the Upper South, with its intellectual center at Richmond, the cult of chivalry achieved its clearest expression. The Old Dominion translated the theme from Abbotsford into an all-pervading way of life, in the class which dominated the scene. Certain local traditions played a role in the process.

The romantic mood had many manifestations in the region led by Charleston and South Carolina. The proud Carolinian aristocrats displayed the trappings of the cult of chivalry as though they were a badge of Southernism. And among these sophisticated people there developed the most ambitious romantic manifestation of the antebellum period—the idea of Southern nationalism.

A third romantic pattern took form in the Gulf South, which looked to New Orleans for intellectual guidance. Here, too, the cult of chivalry was important, though colored with a touch of Gallic gaiety. The quest of New Orleans for commercial grandeur, with its concomitant adventures in Southern imperialism, gave the pattern a distinctive quality.

On the Southwestern frontier still another set of romantic themes emerged. This pattern embraced romantic religion, flamboyant folklore, and a rough version of the chivalric cult.

The single theme common to all four of these patterns was the Southern cult of chivalry. It permeated the region of Richmond influence; it clothed the political philosophy brought to maturity in Charleston; it blended with the commercial ambitions and the convivial life of New Orleans; it was grafted onto the activities of the Southwest with violent possessiveness. It provided the very essence of Southern nationalism.

Sensitive plant though it may seem, the chivalric cult has proved itself the toughest growth in Southern romanticism. It has survived the ancient plantation homes of Virginia, the Confederacy which culminated the Carolina idea of Southern nationalism, the dreams of economic dominance that once fired New Orleans, and the complex of frontier romanticism which flourished in the Southwest.

It has even outlived those "two legs of the tripod" —the plantation system and the institution of slavery, although elements of both these may have persisted "in modern dress." It is the surviving atavism of antebellum civilization, continuing down into the present day. The cult of manners still exerts a rigid rule in Dixie and the place of woman is not that sought by Susan Anthony and Carrie Chapman Catt. "Southern oratory" is a phrase with contemporary validity; and so is "Southern hospitality." If the center of the military cult has departed from Virginia, it is now to be found "Deep in the Heart of Texas." It is true that the duel is pretty well outlawed, but there are substitutes available when "Southern honor" is assailed and "Southern blood" runs hot.

Akin to this persistent cult of chivalry is the chief legacy of Southern romanticism to the post-1865 history of the United States—the cult of the Lost Cause. The romantic dream of the Confederacy and the glamorous picture of the knights who rode for its glory are treasured possessions of the American people. The epitome of Southern romanticism is Battle Abbey at Richmond, where the flag of the Lost Cause still floats proudly and where the walls are filled with heroic murals depicting Lee and his lieutenants in the great day of the Confederacy. . . .

Once romantic themes were admitted past the cordon sanitaire, they were more thoroughly absorbed into the life of the people than in any other civilization of the nineteenth century. Others read the *Waverley Novels* with enthusiasm but the South sought to live them. Romantic nationalism fired repressed groups everywhere. The South not only fought an all-out war over it but has cherished the dream of the Lost Cause ever since. Intensity, also, marked the New Orleans quest for commercial grandeur and the romantic themes of the Southwestern frontier.

Southern romanticism was a major factor in shaping the antebellum civilization. An understanding of its nature, therefore, is essential to an understanding of that civilization.

The themes identified with Southern romanticism performed several specific functions. The idea of Southern nationalism supplied the one remaining solution to preserving the Southern way of life, after such preservation seemed no longer possible within the framework of the Union. Romantic religion and flamboyant folklore both had utility in bringing satisfaction, sociability, and entertainment to frontier life. The quest for commercial grandeur, at New Orleans, stimulated economic activity.

As for the cult of chivalry, it may have provided, as W. J. Cash maintained, an escape from a guilt complex over slavery. More likely, its chief utility was the bringing of color and entertainment into the monotonous routine of rural existence.

Just as cotton and the plantation system, on the one hand, and the institution of Negro slavery, on the other, were the principal economic and social factors in Southern life, so was romanticism the chief intellectual and emotional factor. Furthermore, the ideas which it sponsored had profound influence in the areas of politics, religion, literature, architecture, economic activity, social structure. . . .

The third leg of the tripod, on which antebellum civilization rested, was Southern romanticism. This included the cult of chivalry as its most persistent manifestation and the idea of Southern nationalism as its most ambitious impulse.

Although contradicting himself on occasion as he spent a lifetime explaining the South to his contemporaries, FRANCIS B. SIMKINS did not allow his inconsistencies to interfere with the publication of his musing about his native region. In this essay he holds that the aristocratic concept has been a compelling factor in the development of the South since the Civil War. He contends that the nation as a whole has assumed that the South was becoming more like the American norm and that southerners have felt it was to their advantage to encourage this myth by assuming a democratic pose. *

Francis B. Simkins

The South's Democratic Pose

The greatest mistake of a leader of the old South was Thomas R. Dew's choice of a European country in which to be educated. The inaugurator of the Pro-Slavery Argument, who was president of William and Mary College, went to Germany instead of to England. Had he gone to England he would have been influenced by a society which proclaimed the virtues of democracy and equality while it practiced social distinctions greater than elsewhere in Christendom. This indulgence in what the French call "Anglo-Saxon hypocrisy" paid off handsomely. The progressive world, kind enough to accept a nation's evaluation of itself, believed the flattering conceit that England was Europe's most democratic country, that King and Lords were stage characters, not the top of a social pyramid.

Had Dew been trained in England, he could have returned home talking of freedom and democracy while covertly accepting the inherited realities of slavery and agrarian aristocracy. Such a shrewd unwillingness to reconcile theory with reality would have led disagreeable Europeans to cry, "Purposeful absentmindedness"; but there is reason to believe that the forces of democracy and liberalism, in their greed for conquest, might not have regarded the Old South as an enemy. The outside world might have been credulous enough to accept the region of slavery according to its profession of democratic sweetness and evolutionary light. The world's evaluation of Thomas Jefferson and Abraham Lincoln proves that this was possible.

Jefferson represented himself as the

---

*Francis B. Simkins, "The South's Democratic Pose," *The Georgia Review*, IV (Winter, 1950), 255–262.

champion of simplicity, equality, and modesty. So successful was this pose that he is accepted as a guide by all advocates of democracy from Wall Street bankers to communists; he is one of the few Americans who cannot be criticized successfully. Yet he was not too simple to live in a Roman mansion instead of in a log cabin and drink madeira wine instead of hard cider. He was not too freedom- and equality-loving to profit by the labor of slaves. He was not too modest to rationalize God into an image strikingly resembling Mr. Jefferson himself.

Abraham Lincoln because of his black beard and white face looked like St. John the Baptist; in proclaiming "Charity to all men" he talked like an humble servant of mankind. At this evaluation he is universally accepted. Yet he was uncharitable enough to wish the Negroes to banish themselves from the land as a condition of their freedom, and was determined to accomplish the great act of national unification over the bodies of thousands.

Dew went to Germany where he learned from Aristotle-inspired professors that all men are not equal and that slavery is as natural as freedom. On coming home he coupled this information with the Bible to justify the keeping of the black man in bondage. Negro slavery, this Southerner asserted, was a necessity of social decency in a community where black men were numerous. There was no hiding of practices and intentions. As applied to the Negro the Jeffersonian doctrine of freedom and equality was denied. Dew and his pro-slavery successors conjured up one hundred arguments to answer the ninety-nine arguments the pundits of democracy were able to collect.

The defenders of the peculiar ways of the Old South were mistaken in believing that they could win the argument through the mere weight of superior logic. The advocates of democracy could use force as readily as reason. They shot down all the targets their pro-slavery antagonists put before them. The South was subjected to the bloodiest assault in modern history before 1914. The region below the Potomac went down in tragic defeat. It paid the penalty of foolishly assuming that revolutionists prating Jefferson believed that truth expressed in words was the most effective weapon against error. Slave-whippers should have known that liberals also can be violent.

The South learned its lesson in 1865. It relegated Dew and his group to the limbo of history and rejoined other Americans in proclaiming the Jeffersonian doctrines which it had professed in the early years of the Republic. This was not enough. To these inherited verities, Southern leaders of the postwar generation added democratic doctrines suited to the new day. They created the myth of the New South by championing universal education and the introduction of Northern industry and Northern ideals of a business civilization. They asserted that the South, in harmony with the benign optimism of Herbert Spencer, would, if given time, shelve its sectionalism and evolve into a happy segment of the great republic in which plutocracy and democracy stood united. Booker T. Washington, the most eminent Southerner of his day, was applauded. He possessed a plan, devious but thoroughly American and materialistic, which promised to raise his race out of the slough of caste into the equality which the Reconstruction experiment had failed to achieve. A Southern congressman was willing to eulogize Charles Sumner. Ex-rebel generals in 1898 were willing to put on the blue uniform and march under the flag they had fought against three decades before. Give the South a bit of the immense time the Victorians allotted to the evolutionary process and it would give up its dark and lackadaisical ways, with only a few magnolias and colonnaded porches left as relics of a benighted past.

Such professions, however, did not square with practice. The statesman who eulogized

Sumner had already broken the jaw of a carpetbagger in the Mississippi county whose dark ways William Faulkner was destined to expose. The South was learning to supplement a revived American patriotism with a fervent reassertion of regional consciousness. It sublimated Jefferson into the aristocrat he truly was. It resented the aspersion that the wife of Andrew Jackson, its most democratic leader, smoked a pipe. It countered Booker T. Washington's optimism by indulging in lynching, job-expulsions, jim-crowing, and disfranchising. It negated the democratic nationalism of the schools by home influences with a Southern bias. It filled the new factory towns with persons as rural in their thinking as those left on the farms. And when, through force bills, office-giving, and civil rights programs, Northern leaders threatened reenactment of the Reconstruction experiment, the South was bitter.

Perhaps the propagandists of post-bellum democracy knew that their words did not reflect the Southern reality. But if they dissimulated, they were lying like the diplomats and gentlemen they were. And they knew that the North was sharing their guilt, even indulging in democratic hypocrisy. They observed that the District of Columbia preferred to lose the sacred privileges of self-government and legislative representation rather than have Negroes participate in the process. They knew that proclamations by New York City and Chicago in favor of race equality were accompanied by the relegation of Negroes to ghettos. They knew that carpetbaggers had not married Negroes and that Yankee schoolma'ams chaperoned so effectively their only successful Southern experiment in interracial education that there were no chances for much interracial familiarities. They knew that the twentieth-century Presidents of the United States did not practice their preachments against race discriminations. They noted that these high officials did not fraternize with Negroes while in the South; that

they failed to appoint Negroes to public office in the South; that they did not invoke the Fourteenth Amendment as the most effective method of frustrating the South's habit of reducing Negro participation in politics to a minimum. Southerners got sardonic delight over the curbs imposed upon a President's wife who awkwardly believed that the discriminations Americans imposed upon thirteen million Negroes should be compared with the discriminations the Germans imposed upon eight hundred thousand Jews.

Oswald Spengler explains the marvelous internal order of the United States in terms of the harmony which exists between plutocracy and democracy. The poor, for reasons that are obvious, admire the rich more than the rich admire themselves. In the South this principle is modified by the substitution of the aristocratic for the money concept.

Historians are disappointed when they look in the Old South for evidences of the Marxian stereotype of the class struggle. They find instead a close conformity by all classes to the concept of broad acres, many slaves, and the colonnaded mansion. The common white man resented Hinton R. Helper's assertion in his *Impending Crisis of the South* (1857) that they were handicapped economically and socially by the planters and the slaves. So odd do Helper's views appear in the environment of the Old South that one historian declared that he was under German influence. The aristocratic consciousness of the white masses of this civilization found unhappy expression in laws of growing rigidity for the control of the slaves and in a dangerous greed for the possession of lands on which they might fulfill their desire to be slaveholders. It found pleasing expression in the sense of mannerliness which pervaded all classes of Southern society.

The aristocratic concept has been so compelling a factor in the development of the New South that it is difficult to discover institutions of wide popular approval of lower-class origin. The most striking exception to this rule is jazz music, an activity started in the Negro quarter of New Orleans and ultimately entering the ball rooms of the rich and the wellborn. Another exception is the leftovers from hog killings such as spareribs and pig's feet which have been metamorphosed by colored cooks into delicacies for the lady's table. A third exception is the mellowing of the corn whisky of the backwoodsman into the bourbon whisky of the gentleman.

The social history of the South is largely the story of the masses imitating the classes. The aristocratic ideal stands, as William J. Cash says in *The Mind of the South,* "perpetually suspended in the great haze of memory, . . . poised somewhere between earth and sky, colossal, shining, and incomparably lovely." It expresses itself in the interests of the thousands of ladies who between the Potomac and the Rio Grande endlessly contemplate their forebears; in the linking of many persons of any degree of sophistication with slave barons; in the penchant in the newer suburbs for domestic architecture which extends beyond colonial Virginia into Tudor England; and in the attraction of hundreds of thousands to Colonial Williamsburg and to Natchez. A primary reason for the failure of the Second Ku Klux Klan is that the upper classes divested the order of its knightly pretensions and exposed it as a clique of barbers, small farmers, and mechanics. An important reason why labor unions have made less progress in the South than elsewhere is that they have never been associated with the upper classes. Pride in social distinctions made the South reluctant to accept woman suffrage. This also has much to do with the fact that the success of the Dixie demagogues was seldom lasting. The South is normally satisfied with political leaders who are gentlemen or at least have gentlemanly aspirations. . . .

Public education is the most widely accorded social privilege of the states of the New South. By 1950 its benefits were extended to all children of both races. Yet it was not the common people who inaugurated this system. It was the dispensation of upper-class agitators and state bureaucrats upon the local communities. Its objective has been the elevation of the common people to aristocratic levels. It imposes cultural standards superior to those of the ancestors.

The Negro, whom Gunnar Myrdal calls an exaggerated American, is the perfect Southerner. He imitates his social superiors among the Southern whites. On winning his liberty, he did not revert to forms of barbarism either American or African. Instead he took the white man's name, his religion, and his social customs. His women developed a passion for finery. He went to schools where his mentors expected him to recover industrial skills in keeping with his humble opportunities; instead he devoted himself to the arts esteemed by the white upper classes.

In the aristocratic aspirations of Southerners are elements of snobbery. In Northern Virginia hunting is practiced in the English style rather than in the style natural to America. Despite broad professions of democracy, Texans are not too humble to imitate the English and Virginians in this respect. The advance of the automobile as the most convenient method of conveyance has not prevented the expansion of horsemanship among the socially ambitious. The growth of the Episcopalian and Presbyterian churches in recent years was caused in part by social advantages accruing to their members. Vast expenditures of the Southern states for education in the humbler trades and professions have not led the carpenter's son to return to the work bench or the farmer's son to return to the plow. Education, if not the means of learning how to get more by doing less, is a means of aspiring after the elevating occupations. The stenographer has learned to dress like the society girl. Golf, once the diversion of the banker, has been taken up by the bank clerk. Football, once only interesting to the college student, is now a main interest of the city workingman.

The Southerner in his actual living accepts the assertion of *The Book of Common Prayer* that there "are all sorts and conditions of men." He could, if he would, justify this attitude by appeals to seers less ancient than Aristotle and the Elizabethans. From modern psychology he could learn that individual differences rather than equality is the rule of nature. From Theodore Dreiser's *An American Tragedy,* as explained by English reviewers, he could learn that something is fundamentally wrong with a society which allows a youth to aspire after a position beyond his training and intelligence. The reason why he hates Soviet Russia is that he sees disadvantages in the extension of social equality into unaccustomed fields; into the fields of wealth, dress and occupations. He could learn that the shortcoming of his expensive school system can be explained partly in terms of applying the same training to all children regardless of actual distinction in talents and backgrounds. He could contemplate the fact that the esthetic barrenness of his section can be explained by the democratic monotony made possible by modern technology and education.

The Southerner could read in both American and European sources the lesson that the key to progress is the existence of an elite. Thomas Carlyle taught it again and again. The Southerner could learn that Europe's great cultural advances from the Renaissance to the present were upper class impositions. Would there, for example, have been an English literature had there been no English aristocracy? He might realize that one of the causes of American progress is the existence of a social ladder which the ambitious person wishes to climb rather than tear down. Take the hierarchy of class away and our free society would disappear; the incentive to pro-

duction would have to be the strap of the policeman on the backs of the serfs of the state.

The Southerner, whatever he may say in his formal moments, does not wish the type of democracy envisaged by the Declaration of Independence and expressed in the Fourteenth and Fifteenth Amendments. Actually he wishes to maintain a caste system more rigid than any which has ever existed in Europe. Why? Because he believes this caste system has been the means of conserving the purity of the white race during the 331 years in which this race has been in contact with the African race. He knows that other white Americans, whatever arguments to the contrary they may gather from anthropology, accept the same view and would therefore jim-crow Southerners were the Southerners to let down the barriers of race. Although he may grant that the anthropologists are correct in asserting the innate mental equality of all races, the Southerner can, with reason, reject race amalgamation on esthetic grounds. He knows that a civilization which values highly both the Greek Aphrodite and the American Bathing Beauty would not look with favor upon a type of woman born of a mixture of the North European stock with the African.

To the South Robert E. Lee is a more precious symbol than Thomas Jefferson. It is the difference between the defeated gentleman in immaculate uniform and jeweled sword and the triumphant democrat who looked like "a tall, large raw-boned farmer" and demonstrated his simplicity by wearing ill-fitting, much worn clothes. This preference makes possible the existence among Southerners of their single unique virtue. It is a certain courtliness of manner which makes all men in a sense into gentlemen. In this attitude is a certain amount of romantic ineffectiveness but in it is room for an ideal of precious worth for a world tending to be dominated by the communist materialism of Asia and the capitalist materialism of the United States.

Why does the South not divest itself of its democratic pretenses about race and class in order to justify its real passion for social distinctions? Thereby it might be at ease with the compelling forces of its ancient heritage. Thereby it might repel the accusation of hypocritical pose and enjoy the comfort of preaching what it intends to do. But the region below the Potomac is not likely to change its evasive habits. It remembers the price of its frankness in 1861. It fears the meddlesome Yankees will use an open confession of sins against Jefferson as a pretext for starting a second Reconstruction. Recent Federal court decisions and Federal legislative proposals give substance to this threat.

These fears should not be so great. Changes which the armies of Grant and Sherman were not able to effect can scarcely be brought about by judicial or legislative ukase. The United States is a federal republic with ingrained sentiments in favor of local determination in matters of intimate concern. Revolutionary changes in the Southern social structure are implied by the plans for Fair Labor Practice and for the abolition of bi-racial schools; they could be made effective only by the change of the United States into a police state. Such absolutism, even to promote the Jeffersonian dream, is not part of the liberal tradition of America. Liberty in this country is held in higher esteem than equality.

JOHN HOPE FRANKLIN (b. 1915) was for several years chairman of the department of history at Brooklyn College, and is now professor of history and chairman of the department at The University of Chicago. A graduate of Fisk and Harvard universities, Franklin is one of the most distinguished Negro historians in the United States. His writings include *The Free Negro in North Carolina* (1943), *From Slavery to Freedom: A History of American Negroes* (1947), and *Reconstruction: After the Civil War* (1961). He is active in the movement to give emphasis in history textbooks to the role of minority groups in American history, and he helped write the brief submitted to the U.S. Supreme Court in the case that produced the landmark school desegregation decision in 1954. In the following selection Franklin argues that ante-bellum southerners had a predisposition toward militancy which went a long way to explain their nineteenth-century actions. *

John Hope Franklin

The Militant South

In 1857, Edmund Ruffin, Virginia's perennial defender of Southern rights, was on the warpath. This time he had good reason to indulge in more than his usual amount of vituperation against the North. There was enough irresponsible talk about the "higher law" and the defiance of the Dred Scott Decision by Northern abolitionists to aggravate even a lukewarm Southerner, and the man who was to fire the first shot at Fort Sumter was not lukewarm. As an elder statesman of the Southern cause, he wrote a series of five articles for the Richmond *Enquirer* and *De Bow's Review*. He poured out his wrath against those who threatened the South and warned that such actions would lead to a disruption of the Union.

Why would the people of the North pursue a course involving such reckless disregard for the future of the nation, Ruffin asked. The answer was that they did so because they lacked respect for the military strength of the South. Consequently, they supposed that they could "vilify and wrong the South to any extent that interest or passion may invite without danger to the North." A decade earlier, "Publicola" of Madison County, Mississippi, had warned Northerners that they "should know enough of Southern character to satisfy them that blustering and bravado are useless, and that the Southern people will at all times be ready to punish any invasion of their rights."

Regarding the character of the South-

*Reprinted by permission of the publishers from John Hope Franklin, *The Militant South*, Cambridge, Mass., The Belknap Press of Harvard University Press, Copyright 1956, by the President and Fellows of Harvard College. Pp. 1–13. Footnotes omitted.

erners, there was almost universal acknowledgment of their remarkable spirit and will
to fight. Indeed, the reputation of the
Southerner's readiness to fight was so well
established that when Northerners spoke
harshly and insultingly of Southern civilization, they could not have been unmindful of
this trait. It might be said that the Southern
hand rested nervously on its pistol, knife, or
sword; and most visitors eyed this threatening
posture with proper respect. Even before the
War for Independence a British traveler in
South Carolina and Georgia observed that
the rural life and the constant use of arms
promoted a kind of martial spirit among the
people, "and the great dangers to which they
were always exposed, habituated them to face
an enemy with resolution." In 1846, the Scot,
Alexander Mackay, described the "fiery
blood of the South." A decade later James
Stirling was disturbed by the proneness to
violence and the readiness to fight which he
observed in the Southern states where "wild
justice easily degenerates into lawless violence, and a bloodthirsty ferocity is developed
among the ruder members of the community."

While the Southern reputation for militancy was viewed with interest and apprehension by some, it aroused considerable criticism and contempt on the part of others.
William H. Russell, correspondent for the
London *Times,* conceded that Southern
gentlemen "travel and read, love field-sports,
racing, hunting, and fishing, are bold
horsemen and good shots. But after all," he
concluded, "their state is a modern Sparta—
an aristocracy resting on a helotry, and with
nothing else to rest upon. . . They entertain
very exaggerated ideas of the military
strength of their little community, although
one may do full justice to its military spirit."
In the practical application of this militancy it
was distressing to Joseph Holt Ingraham to
find violence so completely accepted that no
youngster was entitled to the claims of

manhood "until made the mark of an adver-
sary's bullet." This reputation for fighting
did not always command respect, nor even
serious consideration; but it came to be identified as an important ingredient of Southern
civilization.

Southerners disagreed with many judg-
ments of their way of life, but they never resented the assertion that the martial spirit
was a significant feature of their character.
Thus William Ellery Channing's comment
on the South's impetuousness was praised as
a "finely drawn picture" that displayed "the
hand of the master." Articulate Southerners
promoted the idea of their ferocity, if not
bloodthirstiness. Edward B. Bryan thought
the prospect for successful secession bright
because the Southern fighting spirit was dis-
tinctly superior to the Northern. "As to the
natural military spirit and predilection of the
two people" he said, "we believe that there
can be but little difficulty in reaching a definite conclusion." The pursuits and mode of
life of the Southerners, "joined to their pro-
verbial love of country, create a spirit within
them, which once aroused, never could be
conquered."

What Bryan was saying in 1850, others
had already said and would continue to say
for another decade. Experience in everyday
life had made the Southerner a kind of fighter
unique in the world. His ordinary
amusement was the chase, and as a hunter,
horseman, and rifleman, he was almost naturally trained to war. In a military struggle the
South would surely win, one writer predicted, for it had "more aptitude and genius
for war" than the North. And, having won
the war, Southerners would display great
qualities in their control of the Northern
people. "Naturally generous," another admitted, "Southerners exercise much forbear-
ance, till the question of honor is raised,
and then they rush to the sword . . . fierce and
fearless in a contest, yet just, generous and
gentle in command, they possess every quality

necessary to rule the Northern people . . ." Inheritance was the chief explanation offered by this writer for the military and political superiority of the South. Those who settled the North were "Disaffected religionists," who continued to "carry out the peculiarities of their religion and race." But "the Southern States were settled and governed by persons belonging to the blood and race of the reigning family . . . The Cavaliers directly descended from the Norman Barons of William" were "a race distinguished for . . . war-like and fearless character, a race . . . renowned for . . . gallantry . . . chivalry . . . gentleness, and intellect." That race ruled "the world over, whether the subject be African or Caucasian, Celt or Saxon."

Even Southerners without a claim to cavalier ancestry did not suffer from lack of fighting spirit. Georgians could proudly point to an accumulated tradition of vigor in living and stearnness in their relations with their neighbors and with England that more than compensated for their humble origins. The Scots and Scotch-Irish in the back country brought a tradition of pride, boastfulness, and vigor that found a congenial atmosphere in the frontier environment. The habit of war was ingrained in the Scots; usually their heroes were warriors and their admiration for the qualities of courage, endurance, and loyalty to leaders was almost unbounded.

Thus, articulate Europeans, Northerners, and Southerners had contributed much to the idealization of the Southerner as one of the very fearful characters of the nineteenth century. He enjoyed the reputation of being sensitive, quick to defend his honor, adept and skilled in the use of weapons, and with an inherited capacity to rule the conquered with enviable effectiveness.

The Southerner's reputation as a fighting man rested not only on what others said about him, or even on what he said about himself, but also on what he had *done*. There had been a time when few people were convinced of the South's capacity or will to fight. During the War for Independence, for example, New England patriots feared that their Southern comrades would be derelict in shouldering arms against England. Washington did not exclude the South when he complained of the "dearth of public spirit" in the colonies, and General Charles Lee, in early 1776, was distressed over the lack of enthusiasm and decisiveness in the South. So, too, General Gage anticipated little difficulty with the South. The people in the South "talk very high . . . but they can do nothing. Their numerous slaves in the bowells of their country and the Indians at their backs will always keep them quiet." Few Southerners wrote histories of the War for Independence in the years immediately after the struggle, and Northern writers emphasized the contributions of their section. Southerners remained indifferent to the matter until the intersectional struggle became bitter. In the 1840's, however, they sought not only to establish the unquestioned military superiority of the contemporary Southerner, but also to rehabilitate the gallant Southern fighter for independence.

In *American Loyalists*, Lorenzo Sabine noted this effort to glorify the martial South. "South Carolina," he charged, "with a Northern army to assist her could not, or would not, even preserve her own capital . . ." Southerners who read the book were furious. Outraged, one said that "the claims of Carolina to the distinction which her public men assert may be slurred over by ingenious misrepresentation, but she cannot be defrauded of them . . . We cannot allow that her fame is to be smutched because there were many within her territories with whom her champions were hourly doing battle." In 1850, that eloquent and ubiquitous champion of Southern rights, J. D. B. De Bow, vigorously defended the Southern fighter in the War for Independence. In an address in New York, he asserted that the South, never wanting in chivalrous devotion to the cause,

supplied fully one-third of the yearly enlist-
ments for the war.

From many quarters came defenders of the
South's role. William Martin recalled that
England's defeat in South Carolina resulted
from the heroic sacrifices of the men and
women of that state. Colonel Lawrence M.
Keitt insisted that the Revolution in South
Carolina had been "conceived and organized
by the native population." There might have
been some division, he admitted, "but the
constituted authorities of the State committed
her, from the first, to the Revolutionary
movement, and she neither wavered nor fal-
tered throughout its progress." The argument over the South's valor in the War for
Independence found its way to the floor of the
United States Senate in 1856. In a debate on
slavery, Charles Sumner asserted that the institution had long been a burden to the
country, and taunted Senator Andrew P.
Butler of South Carolina for his state's dere-
liction during this war. South Carolina had
betrayed a "shameful imbecility" as a result
of slavery. The following month Butler, who
had been absent when Sumner spoke, rose to
answer. "I challenge him to the truth of
history," he asserted. "There was not a battle
fought south of the Potomac which was not
fought by southern troops and southern slave
holders . . ." Indeed, South Carolina had
given as much to the cause as Massachusetts.

In the 1850's, the Mecklenburg Declaration, Moore's Creek, Camden, Eutaw
Springs, Kings Mountain, and Yorktown
became major Southern triumphs. In
Southern eyes these landmarks in the achievement of independence had been secured primarily, if not exclusively, by Southern men.
Doubtless these experiences had stimulated
the South's martial spirit. The sheer inadequacy of its defenses at the outbreak of the
war with England had been terrifying to contemplate. Just before the war an Englishman
said that Charleston, the most fortified town
in the South, had only three "apologies for

Fortifications," and that the "Common
Town Militia if possible make a worse Figure
than the Train Bands of London." Later,
Southern writers were to speak of the lack of
defenses in their section, the inadequacy of
the support from Philadelphia, and the "se-
verity and frequency of her fields of fight."
Indeed, the bitter experiences during the siege
of Charleston and the ignominious defeat at
Camden were not soon to be forgotten.
Southerners could well have decided that
thereafter they should keep their powder dry
and keep plenty of it.

In the War of 1812 the South's fighting
reputation made substantial headway. The
promoters of the war were, for the most part,
Southerners, and nowhere was there more
enthusiastic support of the war than in the
South. Southern militia were early placed on
a war footing, while New England's governors were defying the federal government's call for men. To one Virginian this
seemed the blackest of crimes and in his re-
monstrance he cried:

> O! Good people of New England! Pause!
> Pause! for heaven's sake, pause! Stand a moment
> on the brink and look at the great ocean of trouble
> before you embark or you may be lost amidst the
> storms of the deep . . .

Meanwhile in Baltimore, where an editor
dared to criticize the war, a mob sacked and
virtually destroyed his offices. Southerners
easily possessed the greater will and anxiety
to fight. David Campbell of Richmond expressed the views of many when he said that
he had a most "prodigious fever to put on the
armour of a soldier . . . to bear a part in a
glorious and honorable war waged for the liberty and happiness of man . . ."

The Mexican War gave Southerners an
opportunity to display their gallantry in
battle and to advance their economic and political interests. As early as 1845, this "magnificent dream of sport, glory and opulence
seemed to be on the point of realization, and

the war spirit flamed high." The Richmond *Enquirer,* its ardor for war overflowing, asked, "What more inspiring strain can strike the ears of freemen than the trumpet note which summons our people to the punishment of tyrants?" The New Orleans *Picayune* observed that wherever one went in that city the talk was of "War and nothing but war." When war came, the enthusiastic support of the Southern states completely eclipsed the rather feeble martial activity in other parts of the country. Thomas R. R. Cobb of Athens, Georgia, wrote his brother Howell, in Congress, that he "never saw the people more excited. A volunteer company could be raised in every county in Georgia." Tennessee answered the call for 3,000 men with 30,000. North Carolina offered more than three times her quota. In Savannah, so many volunteer companies sought to represent the city that had been asked to send one company that it was deemed necessary to decide by lot which organization should be accorded the honor.

The gallant men of Mississippi thought that Governor Albert G. Brown was much too slow in putting the state on a war footing. The Natchez Fencibles marched to Jackson and burned the governor in effigy before his mansion. A fighting bard, who might have been motivated by political considerations, expressed the same feeling in a local paper:

> Our Gov'ner has betrayed his trust
> He has disgraced our name
> And for his treacherous acts we have
> Condemned him to the flame.
>
> Alas! let this hereafter be
> A warning to the rest
> We love a brave and valiant man
> A coward we detest.

The war's impact on the South was remarkable, and the fighting zeal of the Southern people was incomparable. Almost everywhere men deserted peaceful pursuits for the battlefield. Charles Lanman said that many households in the Allegheny region had been "rendered very desolate by the Mexican War." When the call was issued for volunteers, the men of the Southern mountains "poured into the valley almost without bidding their mothers, and wives, and sisters a final adieu . . ." The men of Mississippi were outraged when three regiments from Tennessee, "whose people were neither braver nor better," received a call while Mississippi men still waited. One planter viewed the great enthusiasm for war as having, ironically enough, a real social significance. "The war," he wrote, "will serve one good purpose—thin out loafers. In Natchez there is quite a patriotic spirit amongst such folk."

The victories gave the South an excellent opportunity to claim a superior will to fight, and it missed no opportunity to do so. After the battle of Buena Vista, Charles Dabney, a student at the College of William and Mary, wrote his parents, "we may all be proud to say that we are Mississippians. Look at the veteran coolness with which they received the charge of the Mexican cavalry. Look at the Southern impetuosity with which they threw themselves into every dangerous position." To illustrate the South's superior military strength, James De Bow published a summary of the contribution of the North and the South to the war: 43,000 Southerners and 22,000 Northerners took part in the struggle. Louisiana contributed seven times as many men as Massachusetts; Tennessee sent more than 5,000 men, while New York sent less than 1,700.

When Thomas Nichols made his first visit to New Orleans, he saw the returning heroes thrilling the crowds. In the Place D'Armes a military band was playing. The artillery company, going through its evolutions, was a further demonstration of the "pomp and circumstances of glorious war." In 1859 the Mississippians were still praising the valor of their men in the war. "As long as American arms and valour shall be honored, or the American name be known," William Crane pronounced, "so long will the First Mississippi Regiment and Jefferson Davis be remembered and admired by every chivalric son of Mississippi."

Some Southerners discerned a far-reaching significance growing out of their performance in the Mexican War. One thought that it proved the Southerners competent to engage in foreign conquest. "It has shown that, in foreign invasion we are wanting in none of the elements which enable us to maintain our liberties at home." The really significant thing, however, was the way in which the war enhanced the South's military reputation.

As a military people, none can deny that we are fully equal, perhaps superior, to any other. Our renown for skill, courage, and indomitable energy in battle, humanity and moderation after victory, has overspread the world . . . and the storm of war which shook Mexico to her foundations, roused not the slightest ripple upon the smooth waters of our internal repose.

By 1860 the South claimed to be the fountainhead of martial spirit in the United States. It argued that it had turned the tide of battle in the nation's wars and had been the training ground for the soldiers of the country. America's soldiers had even been schooled in the art and science of war by treatises written by Southerners. Major D. H. Hill boasted that the Southern scholar had evinced the section's military spirit just as forcefully as had the soldier. "The books on Infantry Tactics we use, were prepared by Scott, of Virginia and Hardee, of Georgia. The Manual of Artillery Tactics in use is by Anderson of Kentucky. The only works in this country on the Science of Artillery, written in the English language are by Kingsbury and Gibbon of North Carolina." Mordecai of South Carolina was the leading authority on gunpowder, while Mahan of Virginia had published the best works in military

engineering. "These gentlemen are all graduates of West Point and are officers in the Army, but the South claims them as her own."

The South's reputation for fighting—and winning—was secure. This reputation was more firmly established in the minds of Southerners than anywhere else, to be sure; but people in other places took cognizance of the South's claims and were willing to make some concessions regarding its military spirit.

Wars, however, had their limitations in strengthening the military reputation of Southern men, for there were years in which there was no resort to arms against the British, Indians, or Mexicans. But day-to-day experiences kept them in practice. Many were hot-headed and high-tempered, and, in personal relations, conducted themselves as though each were a one-man army exercising and defending its sovereignty. Duels were as "plenty as blackberries" in Mississippi in 1844. Traveling in the Southwest in the 1830's, Ingraham saw and heard about much violence. In new Orleans, "the rage for duelling is at such a pitch that a jest or smart repartee is sufficient excuse for a challenge . . ." What manner of men were these who could refer to an appointment for a duel "with the *nonchalance* of an invitation to a dinner or supper party?"

When there was not dueling, there was fighting. The public walks were arenas for sport among the rustics, most of whom carried weapons and "counted on the chance of getting into difficulty." This violence was described with a mixture of jest and disgust by an Alabama editor:

The Summer Sports of the South, as Major Noah calls them, have already commenced in Huntsville. On Monday last, in the Court Square, and during the session of Court, too, a man by the name of Taylor stabbed another by the name of Ware in such a shocking manner that his life is despaired of . . . this stabbing and dirking business has become so common and fashionable, that it has lost all the horror and detestation among . . . our population . . .

In Florida, Bishop Henry Whipple found the fighting spirit prevalent even among the community's more responsible members. On one occasion a member of the grand jury went outside where he found his son of eight or nine years of age fighting with another boy. "The father looked coolly on until it was ended and then said, 'now you little devil, if you catch him down again bite him, chaw his lip or you never'll be a man.'" The Bishop said that the father's attitude was "only one of the numerous specimens of this fighting spirit only to be found in the South."

The fighting spirit was no respecter of class or race, and the willingness of Negroes to resort to violence shows the extent to which such conduct pervaded the entire community. Free Negroes fought slaves, whites, and each other. Fearful of losing the few privileges that freedom accorded them and dogged by the vicissitudes that the struggle of such an anomalous position involved, they frequently outdid other members of the community in manifesting a proclivity to fight. There were fights among slaves and revolts and rumors of revolts. Owners and overseers, moreover, occasionally met foul play as they undertook to supervise and punish their slaves. The people of Louisiana were excited in 1845 over the murder of a Caddo Parish mill superintendent by a Negro whom he sought to chastise. What was more, the *New Orleans Bee* complained, "instances of this kind are becoming quite numerous. It was only a few months since that a Negro was hanged in Greenwood for attempting the life of his overseer; and but a few weeks or so since in the . . . County of Harrison, Texas a Mr. Wilson met with the most distressing death by the hand of his own slaves."

Southerners could have done no better job of establishing a reputation for violence and fighting had they sought to do so by formal dramatization. Visitors from the North and from Europe did much to spread the South's reputation for militancy. But the alacrity with which Southerners displayed their bellicosity and the boastful pride with which they discussed it contributed significantly to the general impression that Southerners were a pugnacious lot. They were not being merely theatrical, although they had their moments of sheer acting. The flow of blood and the grief produced suggest a deep, pervading quality that could not be overlooked. Violence was inextricably woven into the most fundamental aspects of life in the South and constituted an important phase of the total experience of its people.

Fighting became a code by which men lived. Southerners themselves were apt to explain their dueling and other fighting propensities by pointing to the aristocratic character of their society; but this explanation seems somewhat flattering. The aristocratic element was much too inconsequential to give a tone of manners to the whole community; and the widespread existence of violence, even where there was no semblance of aristocratic traditions, suggests influences other than those of the select. The prevalence of violence was due, in part at least, to the section's peculiar social and economic institutions and to the imperfect state of its political organization. The passions that developed in the intercourse of superiors and inferiors showed themselves in the intercourse with equals, for, observed Stirling, "the hand of the violent man is turned against itself." Far from loathing violence, the man of the South was the product of his experiences as a frontiersman, Indian fighter, slaveholder, self-sufficient yeoman, poor white, and Negro. He gladly fought, even if only to preserve his reputation as a fighter.

A thought-provoking extension of John Hope Franklin's contention that men of the Old South had a penchant for militancy has been made by FRANK E. VANDIVER (b. 1925), who maintains that "reaction to challenge" best explains the South of the twentieth century as well as of the nineteenth. The essay below was originally delivered at the University of Judaism in Los Angeles as one of a series of lectures on "Extremes in American Life." Professor of history at Rice University, Vandiver is an authority on the Confederacy and the military history of the Civil War. He has written *Ploughshares into Swords: Josiah Gorgas and Confederate Ordnance* (1952), *Rebel Brass: The Confederate Command System* (1956), *Mighty Stonewall* (1957), and *Jubal's Raid* (1960).*

Frank E. Vandiver

The Southerner as Extremist

Southerners are, and have been portrayed in various guises: arrogant, cheroot-puffing planters, sipping juleps; power-sodden, leisure-ridden fops, watching in slack-jawed pleasure the beating of a slave; dirt-grubbing sharecroppers, hating their debts to the country store; anonymous amalgams of men, faceless and pale behind their sheets, burning crosses, lynching fellow men; money-worshipping scalawags, grasping the trough of the Great Barbecue; gross politicos, bellowing racist catechisms with Bilbo-like fervor; indignant men of liberal stripe, the James Petigrus, the Hodding Carters, the Ralph McGills, fighting lonely, dirty battles; masses with hate-contorted faces, screaming at television cameras, frothing on schoolyards in Little Rock, New Orleans, Oxford.

No matter the guise, one underrunning trait brands them all: violence. Far back in the history of the South visitors and natives alike noted a violent strain as an integral part of Southern character. "Wild justice easily degenerates into lawless violence," one observer noted in the 1850's, adding that a "bloodthirsty ferocity is developed among the ruder members of the community."

The gentry, however, were by no means immune to extremism. No other part of the country sported as many devotees of the code duello and its attendant protocols of chivalry. Real and fancied sallies against a man's honor required satisfaction, and a quick pistol or deft foil guaranteed an unsmirched reputation. True dandies might boast several victims—pinked if not dispatched. Such personal redress of grievances received the blessing of custom well into the first half of the nineteenth century. Southerners regarded individual bravery as part of a man.

Bravery and physical courage came to be so vital a part of the "Southern way of life" that they were paraded at every opportunity. Where legitmate opportunities were scarce, special ones were often staged for displays of bravado and derring-do. Tournaments of a medieval character were sometimes held, with balanced cavaliers atop Arabian charges doing battle for a lady's favor.

Such belligerent courage, such bellicose honor, can easily warp into senseless bullying, given the proper circumstances. The proper circumstances existed in the South. A frontier civilization which grew in waves of westward settlement, the South developed a rustic cast reinforced by abundant, thinly settled land. Rustics are normally fiercely independent, industrious folk, jealous of rights and chattels. Southerners had all these traits, but they were conditioned by one constant peculiar to the South: slavery. The slave system in its economic, political, and social implications added an intangible something to the violent strain running strong in Southerners.

Although the traditional idealization of Dixie as a happy land of moonlight, magnolias, and jollifying pickaninnies has faded before history, there is some truth in it. And there is some truth, too, in the other side of the idyl—the side of misery, fear, and Simon Legree. Power does indeed corrupt and never so surely as when exercised directly over men. Slaves were at the mercy of their masters, and while some Southern states boasted legal limits to an owner's authority, in practice he could do almost as he wished with his property. Weak men, prurient, sadistic, impious men with such power often yielded to temptation. At its worst, slavery became a Negro purgatory, with slaveowners, slave drivers, and overseers twisting bravery into bestiality

in orgies of lashings, beatings, and humiliations. Certainly these were exceptions to a general rule of humane and careful treatment, but exceptions which carried the violent strain.

The strain may be glimpsed in other ways. As John Hope Franklin shows in *The Militant South,* the section devoted much time to martial matters. Military schools, militia units, elite guard companies flourished below Mason and Dixon's line. Southern men claimed prowess in the field, boasted their outdoors stamina, their custom to the saddle, their skill with guns—all requisites to the frontier and the code of chivalry in the South.

Wars have always fascinated young men of the region, and history has tolled the numbers of those killed, maimed, and blooded in battles for the nation. Southerners fought gallantly (an especially Southern word) at King's Mountain in the Revolution, at New Orleans in 1812, at Buena Vista, Monterey, Chapultepec in Mexico; and a close look will show the large part played by the South in leading the country into these conflicts. Once in the field, Southerners have proved formidable soldiers indeed—often undisciplined, finicky about their rights, suspicious of superiors, but infantry tireless and terrible. Martial pride persists in the Southland.

Politics persist, too, and as politicos Southerners have also shown the violent strain. Presumably the slave system gave planters sufficient free time to dabble in government and public affairs; hence they monopolized local offices and dominated party councils. Most Southerners were Democrats (with an occasional stray for sake of appearances), and most took their politics straight. Rural isolation, broken only by infrequent gatherings at county seats or forks of the creek, prescribed a system of personal politicking which suited the situation and the people. Southerners liked nothing better than a rip-roaring stump speaker who fulminated against his rivals with rolling periods and searing invective. A strong, undiluted rhetorical style gave a man character—especially if he aimed it at the character of others.

No one section of the country boasted such relentless zealots for the stump, the smoke-filled room, the ballot box. Southerners were uninhibited, political animals—and to some extent still are.

Even as they cherished political fundamentalism, so, too, they cherished religious fundamentalism. God counted in Dixie. He counted in various ways, of course, according to persuasion, but in the Old South religion had a large part in daily life. People in the frontier areas, remote from eastern decorum, believed in a personal God, sought His favor, prayed with fervor and conviction. Religion came stronger to Southerners, doubtless because most of them lacked the sophistication of brethren in the North's Burnt-over District. Preachers, be they Methodist, Presbyterian, or Baptist (Episcopalians and Catholics were less demonstrative), rode their camp meetings, their circuits, or their pulpits fervidly and carried the Word with bombast sufficient to match the glibbest politician. Hell loomed real and awful every Sunday; brimstone billowed and burned; salvation came only with purging and penitence—and those who backslid or wandered from the path were branded by the lash of biblical oratory. Not all denominations, of course, pursued fundamentalist masochism, but even among sedate congregations in the South religion had stronger flavor than elsewhere. It still does.

This strain of violence, present in so many facets of the Southerner, might never have amounted to more than a dangerous crotchet had not a focus, a direction, been given it. Direction, purpose, if you will, came largely from the fact that the South developed along almost Hegelian lines. By this I mean that its character, its mores, its reactions, its violence, evolved in response to external (and sometimes internal) challenges. As things worked out, the South could never quite achieve a synthesis, for it usually failed to meet a challenge with the proper response. It attempted always to react, but in so doing, it often over-acted. . . .

Let me say that I agree that the South was, is, and probably will be, different from the rest of the country. I do not think that difference is necessarily evil. But I do suggest that response to challenge is a theme in Southern experience which is perhaps more constant than others. . . . It focuses the deep currents of extremism in Southern blood, it explains the political, social, military, even economic behavior, and—to me, at least—it comprehends the South.

For my purposes, let me call this pattern of reaction to challenge the offensive-defense mechanism. I like this term, not only because I am a student of military history, but also because it is Jefferson Davis' own and hence has the best possible imprimatur!

To begin: It seems to me that the first clear-cut use of the Southern offensive-defense mechansim occurred in 1798 and found expression in the Virginia and Kentucky Revolutions. True, the South itself sustained no attacks in 1798, but Virginia and Kentucky expressed a lurking fear of federal encroachment on the Constitution which might lead to later oppression. Most important to the future of the South was the reaffirmation by Kentucky in 1799 of its objection to federal infringement and its assertion of nullification as a legitimate weapon against the "general government." Implicit in all these resolutions was the principle of state review of the Constitution and of federal legislation. This principle, worked finally into the doctrine of interposition, still beguiles the South.

For a time in the early nineteenth century Southern extremism took a firm nationalistic path. Such leaders as Clay and Calhoun labored to strengthen and unify the United States—even to the extent of preaching a jingoistic crusade against England in 1812. Gradually history appeared to work against the South's equal place in the Union, despite the luster of the Virginia dynasty. As far as the South could see, two ugly stains spread slowly across the image of the nation: industrialism and abolition. In the early years of the nineteenth century industrialism and its parasitic bureaucracy caused the greatest concern, but with the Missouri Compromise abolitionism came to a lingering, ominous prominence. These dual threats—unbridled capitalism spreading industry and federalism inexorably across the country; fanatical abolitionists striving to destroy the South's economic and social order—these threats demanded counterattack.

Initially the offensive-defense seemed moderate enough. Southern leaders worked for the Missouri Compromise, but for a highly sectional reason: they sought a chance to expand the South. Expansion figured prominently in Southern plans, since additional Southern states were essential to keeping a balance between the North and South in the Senate. If the agrarian system could expand westward below the line 36° 30′, the perilous balance might be maintained and Northern nationalist and abolitionist legislation blocked. If the balance slipped, agrarian democracy was doomed along with slavery.

Clearly, though, the tide of Western civilization ran hard against Dixie. Try as it might, the South simply could not keep pace with Northern economic and political expansion. Cotton's kingdom looked prosperous enough at a casual glance, and the growing monopoly of world markets reinforced the illusion. Shrewd businessmen, though, and practiced judges of Southern economics, urged diversification and argued that agriculture could hardly stand alone. The South found itself caught in a trap of history—long addiction to staple production tied the planter to a factorage lien system and this, in turn, made diversification virtually impossible. Circumstances pushed the whole section steadily toward an almost mystical cotton idolatry.

Cotton proved a jealous idol. Grown in increasing abundance, it demanded expanding markets, consequently Southerners relied heavily on European trade. This made them especially uneasy about the effects on the price level of the federal tariff policy. The tariff question has all but disappeared from textbooks, but before the Civil War it ranked as one of the biggest snags in the fabric of union. After several incidents the controversy boiled over in 1832, following the passage of the ill-famed "tariff of abominations" and its highly protective successor. Southern reaction set in with deadly ferocity and centered in South Carolina (a special study ought sometime be made of why South Carolina blood runs so hot). The upshot of the trouble was nullification, nullification according to John C. Calhoun, with genuflection toward the Virginia and Kentucky Resolutions. South Carolina nullified the tariff law; President Andrew Jackson stood firm behind Congress' Force Bill and called the South's bluff. Although Henry Clay managed a compromise tariff which saved everyone's face, the lesson of 1832 could hardly be missed: nullification failed as a counterpoise to creeping federalism. That left only one final, ultimate weapon—secession. Before that last resort, however, many hoped that differences might be reconciled within the framework of the Constitution.

Southerners had long paraded their passion for the Constitution, and certain it is that they became the most legalistic of Americans. This led them to develop an elaborate constitutional argument as a kind of intermediate line of defense; strict constructionist dogma might make secession unnecessary.

It might have worked, save for a new issue arising in the 1840's, an issue beyond the scope of law—this issue was whether or not a slaveowner could take slaves into federal territories. Southerners saw no problem, of course, since private property could be taken anywhere in the country and enjoy protection of the laws. To the extent that they saw things, the Southerners were right. Their conception of the situation overlooked the fact, however, that many Northerners wanted to restrict slavery's spread. So the real issue came down to freedom versus slavery, free soil versus slavocracy. The whole touchy business was aggravated by the activities of New England emigrant aid societies, which poured money and settlers into Kansas and Nebraska in the 1850's. Again the offensive-defense: Southern groups rushed in a counterwave of emigrants to balance the scales. Skirmishing between both sides erupted into full-scale battles, and the bloody war in Kansas ran luridly across the nation's headlines throughout the decade.

Sadly for the South, the Kansas counterthrust proved too weak to restrict free soil. The appeal of free soil seemed irresistible. Even the spectacular court victory proclaimed in the Dred Scott decision of 1857 could not dim the portent of free soil's relentless spread.

Compromise, tried by both protagonists, narrowly averted a breach in 1850. The keystone of Henry Clay's compromise was a new Fugitive Slave Act; on its strict enforcement depended Southern acceptance of the entire package. But almost immediately various states north of Mason and Dixon's line began a campaign to nullify the act—they adopted the Personal Liberty Laws which gave freedom to all within their borders.

Such laws, of course, abrogated Clay's compromise, but the South stayed its violence for a time and sought protection under the Constitution. But there was almost no Northern co-operation and hence no protection under the law. This ultimate failure came at a tender time, for it showed clearly how hollow was the Dred Scott decision and pointed up the moral strength of the North's new Republican party.

Denied the Constitution, badgered by ceaseless abolitionist propaganda, the South wrapped itself in a burgeoning nationalism, and, reinforced by its conviction of slavery's "positive good," fell back on its last resort: secession.

Few responsible Southerners seriously advocated separation; most regarded it as a dangerous expedient to be avoided at virtually all costs. But the costs had finally mounted too high; the time had come at last to take the offensive against Yankee thraldom, to withdraw from a country without justice.

In the case of the Civil War the South took the offensive by seceding, the North reacted by resisting disunion, and the South then had to react to a war of unprecedented anger. Time would show the war as much more than a brothers' conflict, would make it a cleavage in life for the South. Beyond battles and dying and heroics, it became a kind of ultimate confrontation of the North, of civilization, of time itself. To this mysteriously fundamental struggle the South committed every man, every sinew; its tatterdemalion gray ranks never had enough men, food, guns, bullets, shoes, or medicine, but they held back history for four years.

Everything went with the war—energy, hope, blood, treasure. Sated with death and privation, Southern violence lay dormant through the early years of Reconstruction; dormant, but not dead. And it may well be that the greatest tragedy of Reconstruction is that it revitalized the violent strain through the real and fancied excesses in the "late rebel states." Instances of Yankee oppression and brutality brought on the old offensive-defense mechanism, that conditioned response which even the Civil War could not kill.

The initial Southern reaction aimed more at keeping a distinct place in the nation rather than at suppressing the black man. But the efforts of Radical leaders to put the "bottom rail on top" in Dixie, to deny whites any part in government while elevating the Negro to a status for which he was mentally and emotionally unprepared, produced resentment. Tragically, the Negro became the symbol of Southern degradation, the "cause of it all." Reaction focused on him, as dread bands of "ghosts" ranged the Southern countryside, first terrifying, then burning, flogging, scourging. Violence mounted as the Klansmen rode. Before this savage current ebbed again, misery and terror spanned the old Confederacy.

Oddly enough, Klan terrorism marks one of the few times the Southern offensive-defense mechanism won a victory. Radical Reconstruction doubtless faded for many reasons, but Southerners could argue from tangible evidence that their defiance brought salvation. So the violent strain fed on success.

After 1877 and the final "redemption" of the South, white supremacy did, indeed, become the hallmark of the section —that and a passion for the Yankee dollar. Violence could rest for a time since white rule was easily maintained by an occasional burning cross and the specter of the Klan.

The offensive-defense took a slightly different form through the 1880's and 1890's. Efforts centered on keeping conservative Democrats in power, on chilling supporters of radical farm and labor movements, on building a politically and socially solid South. Southern politicians found racist extremism a usefull weapon in these campaigns. The time-worn catechism of "a white man's country" proved as persuasive as the tattered "Bloody Shirt."

Such wholehearted concentration on political control resulted in a kind of Southern isolationism which allowed the section to lapse into economic decay. Behind the cotton and racist curtains, procrustean leaders sought a split-level prosperity—one which would fatten the rich and starve the poor. They boasted the virtues of balanced budgets (achieved through such economies as truncated public school systems) and no public

debts (achieved in some cases through repudiation), while living on Yankee capital induced to the South with promises of cheap land and labor. Forgotten in their stagnating enclave, Southern Bourbons built a shabby record of irresponsibility—and I say this despite some recent efforts to erect their perfidy into principle.

Isolation can breed conformity. It did in the South. And conformity, in a way, fitted into the pattern of offensive-defense. When next invoked, around the turn of the century, the mechanism focused on elements of unrest in the South itself. Populism and other radical isms posed threats to the status quo and had to be suppressed. Suppression was accomplished first by skilful brandishing of white supremacy and later, when unions loomed seriously, by tarring some of the labor movements with a Bolshevik brush.

Neglected and almost forgotten by the rest of the country, the South had few outlets for its violence for some years. But there had to be outlets—they were demanded by Southern nature. Fortunately some of the violence could be expended in legitimate ways. In 1898, for example, war with Spain offered a chance for another Southern crusade, and the whole section burned with martial ardor. And so it did during World War I, when Southern prowess at arms won added fame in the heroics of the dauntless Dixie Division.

Following World War I, at a time when the violent strain surely was sated with blood, the South continued along its poverty-ridden course. In the midst of the Great Depression the section ranked as the most depressed part of a depressed country. At first glance it seems miraculous that so little extremism occurred in the South in the 1930's, but it ceases to be surprising when the long history of penury is remembered. What violence there was during the depression had a familiar look. Textile workers, driven by unbearable privation, went on strike in some Southern mills. And wherever there was a strike, there was almost always violence. Irate fellow Southerners, traditionally dedicated to laissez faire, rioted in support of mill owners. Anyone who upset the time-honored order of things was un-Southern!

Negro workers always got the worst of the trouble, especially so during the depression. Lowest paid, they were the first to be fired. In the labor troubles of the early thirties they received the brunt of the violence. This was hardly new; the Klan had shaped the pattern of Negro persecution fifty years earlier, and the South followed it with increasing dedication. Even in the days of splendid isolation, the Negro knew no "salutary neglect." Shocking statistics on lynchings can be offered to show savagery bubbling to Dixie's placid surface in the half-century following Reconstruction. Diseases of all kinds, social, economic, political, found remedy in a good lynching, and resort to the hanging tree became a kind of Southern tribal rite. Some thought that spilling a little colored blood now and then might be a good thing for the South. Obviously it was the worst possible thing, and there were many people, increasingly many, who said so and worked to disband the necktie parties. But lynchings were symptoms, symptoms of latent uncertainty, hostility, and, most of all, fear. I think they represent a distinct facet of the offensive-defense mechansim, one that could be glimpsed in the earlier Klan activities and the threats of violence. They served notice on the Negro that he would remain inferior and on his Northern encouragers that the South would not be made over in Yankee image, would not lose its identity to onrushing bureaucracy.

To some extent the problem of Negro participation in Southern life had been assuaged by the famous *Plessy* vs. *Ferguson* decision in 1896. Separate but equal public facilities created an illusion of equality and fixed the condition of second-class citizenship on the Negro. Jim Crow practice spread until Negroes moved automatically to the rear of anything, and crippling subservience marred the manhood of their race.

It is true that tranquillity at length prevailed south of Mason and Dixon's line. The depression must take the credit for much of it, the Northern "hands-off" for some, and a true affection between black and white for the rest. Affection between the races is hard for present-day liberals to swallow. Herbert Aptheker, a modern historian, sees class warfare as constant between blacks and whites, finds incipient Negro revolts behind each headline, and looks toward a Marxist millennium to save the situation. The Progressive School of American historians, currently ascendant, sees only evil in slavery and segregation and doubts any shred of the myth about whites and blacks loving one another. Some did and some still do. May they increase!

Current tensions certainly started with the case of *Brown* vs. *Board of Education of Topeka* in May, 1954. This historic, long-overdue decision sought to redeem an unfulfilled promise of the Civil War. As C. Vann Woodward has perceptively said, the North had three war aims: first to save the Union; second, to free the slave; third, to honor the pledge of equality proclaimed in the Declaration of Independence. The third war aim had not been achieved, but the promise had never lapsed.

On that fateful day in 1954, many Southerners believe, the tortuous progress in race relations (and they can point to some remarkable achievements during the last thirty years) stopped. The Supreme Court decision burst on the South as another external threat, almost as a neo-abolitionist attack. The long struggle was over; the North still pursued its course toward complete, absolute domination.

Instantly the South reacted with the offensive-defense. The caption of the mechanism had always been: "We want to be left alone; you people up North don't understand our situation because you don't have

Negroes in large numbers." But by 1954 things had changed, and the statement had no shred of truth to it. Negroes, segregation, and racial tensions were common in Northern cities, and relations between whites and blacks were often worse than in the South. So this new Yankee assault must be aimed not at uplifting the Negro but at destroying the identity of the South. What was it about the South the Yankee envied enough to hate?

Whatever the North's objective, the South needed a new battle cry to rally its defense. When it came, it had an ageless appeal, but also a viciousness missing before: "No integration, no mongrelization, no social degradation." The proud purity of the Anglo-Saxon was at stake now; school integration would obviously lead to social mixing; that, to miscegenation.

Direct action against the Court's decision built up slowly, with moderate voices raised in caution. The Klan was dead, or at least moribund, for which decent opinion in the South gave thanks, but the odious White Citizens Councils arose to lead the new offensive. . . .

Extremism, in the long run, could not be denied. Demogoguery is a phase of it, and the Citizens Councils' demagogues rose to rant once again about the white man's country, the old order, the evils of Yankee aggression. . . .

Southerners cannot change their spots or alter their chemistry. Land, climate, and blood will make them in future as hot-tempered and quick to resentment as ever. They will continue to rely on the offensive-defense mechanism, and it will probably cause as much trouble as it has in the past. But it is important to remember that the mechanism is triggered by aggravated provocation. Once this is realized, the Southern extremist makes sense.

Although best known for his work on Reconstruction in Texas, where he taught for thirty-five years at the University of Texas, CHARLES W. RAMSDELL (1877–1942) devoted the last twenty years of his life to research and writing about the Southern Confederacy. Several penetrating articles and a book entitled *Behind the Lines in the Southern Confederacy* (1944) constitute the basis for a better understanding of the region and its relationship to the nation as a whole. In this essay published in 1934, Ramsdell points up the importance of agriculture and agrarian ways in the South's history. *

Charles W. Ramsdell

Preoccupation with Agriculture

The dominant factor in the history of the South has been its preoccupation with agriculture and especially with the great staple crops of cotton, tobacco and sugar. Despite the rapid growth of cities and the development of mechanic industries in recent years, the bulk of the population is still primarily concerned with the cultivation of the soil. The economic and social status of the agricultural classes, therefore, has largely determined both the conditions of southern life and the patterns of thinking. But the regional situation has long been complicated by other factors. In the first place there is the race problem, which was deeply involved in the southern defense of slavery and, far from being eliminated, was made more difficult by

the emancipation of the blacks. Another factor which has had much influence upon the regional attitude, one which developed before 1860 and was emphasized by conditions after Appomattox, was the consciousness that the South was a sectional minority, relegated to a subordinate position in national affairs, and that it must be constantly on the defensive against the policies of the rich and powerful North. And of far-reaching importance, in both its social and its psychological consequences, was the blighting poverty which was inflicted upon the whole region by the Civil War and the ensuing decline of agriculture. Even now, two-thirds of a century after the debacle of 1865, although the South has recovered much lost ground, it has not regained

---

*Charles W. Ramsdell, "The Southern Heritage," in W. T. Couch (ed.), *Culture in the South* (Chapel Hill, N.C.: University of North Carolina Press, 1934), pp. 1–15, 17–23.

a position of importance in national life comparable to that which before 1850 was the foundation of its sectional pride.

The differences between North and South, based on soil and climate, began far back in colonial days, but they were not great enough at that time to cause friction. Both sections were concerned chiefly, though not in the same degree, with agriculture and trade. It was not until the opening years of the nineteenth century that their interests began sharply to diverge. It was then that the industrial revolution began to change the economic organization of New England and the middle states, while through its textile machinery and the cotton gin it suddenly made raw cotton a staple of the world market and turned the agriculture of the lower South in a new, profitable and fatal direction.

While mills and factories multiplied and capital concentrated in the North Atlantic states, eager farmers and planters along the coast and far into the back country of the Carolinas and Georgia were growing cotton and dreaming of larger estates and greater profits. High prices for the raw staple made fortunes for successful planters and the "cotton craze" spread to all classes. After the War of 1812 a steady steam of settlers moved into the new Gulf states, cleared the forested lands along the rivers, and by 1830 were producing over half of the total crop. The development of this new southwest was phenomenal, but it is easily explained. Cotton was not only a reliable cash crop, since it sold readily in the world market, it was also normally the most profitable of all crops on good soil. Above all, it was well suited to large-scale production with Negro slave labor. Slaves, in fact, were essential to large planting units; for the task of clearing the thickly wooded river lands and carrying on the routine of new plantations required constant labor. A steady and adequate supply of free white labor could not be procured on this frontier where even the poorest white man

could always get land to cultivate for himself. The large landowner must have Negroes or leave his fields unplanted. The successful cotton grower found that the most promising investment for the profits from his crop was in more land and more labor. It was, in fact, almost the only one open to him. Thus the plantation system continued to expand and the lower South was committed to cotton and to slave labor by economic forces beyond its control.

The border states were less affected by these momentous changes. Cotton growing made slight headway in North Carolina and Tennessee, and in Virginia, Kentucky and Missouri practically none at all. In these states farmers grew tobacco or hemp, grain and live-stock. They used Negro slaves, but in no such numbers as did the cotton planters to whom they sold their surplus of Negroes. In this upper country, and also in the piedmont and the mountain valleys of the lower South, there was a more diversified industry than in the cotton belt. Difficulties of transportation increased the cost of imported goods and thus made opportunities for local white artisans. Small capitalists erected flour and grist mills where water power was available; others opened coal and iron mines and salt springs; and a few built small yarn and cloth mills. But these were generally local enterprises to supply the local market, and they held their business chiefly because the absence of cheap transportation protected them from outside competition. Richmond, Petersburg, and Louisville became small industrial centers, but only because of peculiar local advantages. Meanwhile these enterprises had little effect upon the general trend of southern life, for agriculture and the commerce which it fostered remained the chief concern of the mass of the southern people. . . .

Before 1830 the phenomenal spread of cotton growing into the southwest had brought about a gradual, if fluctuating, decline of prices which began to pinch the planters on the thinner soils of the eastern cotton belt, especially in South Carolina. At the same time the rapid accumulation of banking capital in the industrial and commercial centers of the northeast had enabled northern bankers and brokers to obtain control of the marketing of the crop. Normally the planter shipped his cotton to a commission house or "factor" at the nearest seaport, and from him purchased his yearly supplies. Often the factor was merely an agent for a northern firm which sold the cotton in New England or Liverpool, and subtracted liberally from the proceeds for wharfage, freight, insurance, storage, drayage, and commissions. Whether crops were good or bad, prices high or low, the factors and bankers were able to take their own profits. But the planter found it harder and harder to make a profit from his crops, and the declining trade of Charleston reflected his condition.

Under such circumstances the protective tariff, which had risen steadily since 1816 and had increased the cost of living, was an extreme irritation. The distress in South Carolina was so great by 1832 that her people struck at the tariff through nullification. Although the other southern states refused to endorse the South Carolina remedy, the compromise tariff of 1833 relieved the strain. Andrew Jackson had stopped federal aid of internal improvements in 1832 and destroyed the Bank of the United States in 1836. Agriculture had won the first political battle and it was to win others with the low tariffs of 1846 and 1857; but it had not won the campaign. The northern merchant and banker were still taking their accustomed profits from southern trade.

The general economic depression of the late thirties induced a more extensive search for causes and remedies. While some southern planters followed the lead of Edmund Ruffin of Virginia in instituting "agricultural reform" by fertilizing and terracing their fields and rotating their crops, others sought more direct means of breaking their vassalage to northern capital. They had not failed to note that from two-thirds to three-fourths of the total exports of the United States were the products of southern agriculture and that an even larger proportion of the imports came to northern harbors. Since it was evident that northern merchants and bankers paid their accounts in Europe with the country's exports, the planters easily concluded that northern wealth grew largely from the profits of handling southern trade. These profits might be saved to the South. Led by southern merchants, they proposed to cut loose from New York, Philadelphia, and Boston by establishing direct trade with European markets through new lines of steamships and to strengthen this trade by railroad connections between the South Atlantic ports and the Mississippi and Ohio valleys. The great scheme failed because the scarcity of available capital delayed the building of the railroads and because no steamship line could be induced to send ships regularly where freights were seasonal. Northern capital continued to skim the profits from the southern cotton trade.

During the early forties, when the price of cotton fell to ruinous levels, there was much talk of establishing cotton mills in the cotton country. William Gregg of South Carolina and a few other industrial pioneers had pointed the way to success in this direction, and small factories arose along the eastern piedmont from Richmond to Augusta; but because of insufficient capital, inexperience and bad management there were enough failures to discourage investors. When the price of raw cotton rose again men with spare capital turned back to planting—something which they understood and could manage themselves. Nevertheless, the manufacture of yarns and the coarser fabrics made headway, and had they not been set back by the Civil

War, the southern mills might have dominated the industry before the end of the century. In the upper South, Richmond had developed a nucleus of tobacco factories, flour mills, and iron manufactures, while Louisville had for some time been one of the industrial centers of the Ohio valley. But the mass of the southern people continued to till the soil and to exchange at heavy cost their raw produce for northern manufactured goods. As late as 1860 more than ninety per cent of the manufactured products of the United States, exclusive of such things as lumber, turpentine, flour and meal, were fashioned north of the Potomac.

As better times returned in 1850 the planters recovered their confidence in the security of agriculture. The Walker Tariff of 1846 had lowered the cost of manufactured products and southern cotton was in active demand in the markets of Liverpool. There is little doubt that their renewed prosperity was a large factor in winning their acceptance of the great Compromise of that year. What they did not see, or else were unwilling to admit, was that a system of exchanging raw agricultural products for imported manufactures bound the South to a *colonial* economy, and that the results would be the same whether they bought their goods in the North or in Great Britain. Although they exultantly proclaimed with Senator Hammond of South Carolina that "Cotton is King!" they gave evidence of latent uneasiness. They were still irritated that there was no escaping the tribute levied by northern capital and industry, and a small group of irreconcilables began to insist that economic independence could be obtained only by political separation from the overshadowing North. But the economic arguments of the secessionists had little perceptible effect upon the strong sentimental attachment to the Union. Had it not been for the excitement which had arisen over the slavery controversy, it is unlikely that economic grievances alone would have brought the South to disunion. They certainly played a minor part in bringing on the revolt of 1860–1861.

The rapid development of the anti-slavery movement in the North, at the core of which was a virulent and uncompromising demand for immediate and uncompensated abolition, seemed to the southern people a menace far more dangerous than the aggressions of northern capital. It aroused an emotional storm in the South which is hard for most people nowadays to understand. This feeling cannot be attributed wholly to the fear of the loss of the capital invested in slave labor—although that was naturally an important factor—for some of the most determined opponents of abolitionism were men who owned no slaves themselves. It was, in part, a quite natural anger at the rabid accusations and wholesale abuse heaped by the abolitionists upon all men and women who had any connection with the institution or who defended it. And it was, in very large part, a fear of the consequences, if the crusade should prove successful. It must be remembered that when Garrison began the publication of *The Liberator* in 1831 many thousands of Negroes in the lower South were either natives of Africa or were but one generation removed from savagery. As long as these Negroes could be kept under the discipline of the plantation the danger of racial conflict would be minimized; but should they be excited by abolitionist doctrine the consequences might be appalling. Southern men had not forgotten the horrors of the Haiti massacres nor the more recent Nat Turner insurrection in Virginia. To them the abolitionists were fanatical incendiaries, reckless of the lives of the white women and children of the "black belt." For us to say now that the danger of servile uprising was far less than they thought is beside the point. That they believed the danger real is the important fact. On the economic side the abolitionist program threatened not only the loss of capital invested in slaves but also the shrinkage of land values, since it was commonly believed that the Negro could not be depended upon to do much work after he was freed. And it must be remembered that the lands of the slave belt were, on the whole the most fertile in the South. The sum of the matter is that the abolitionist attack seemed to be aimed not merely at the basis of southern economic life but at the existence of white civilization itself. Confronted with these dangers and compelled to listen to lurid descriptions of themselves as monsters of brutality and iniquity, it is small wonder that southern men lost their tempers and therefore lost the power to think objectively on the subject of slavery. The distinction between the abolitionist creed and the milder and much more general form of northern antislavery opinion, which opposed the extension of the institution rather than, as yet, its destruction, seemed to them less and less important; they were convinced that all antislavery sentiment was working around to the abolitionist position. Thrown upon the defensive, they began elaborating a defense of slavery and of everything southern. As the fatal controversy dragged on, every attack from the North deepened the defense patterns in the southern mind. Southern political history during the two decades before secession cannot be understood without taking into account this conviction of being on the defensive and the extreme sensitiveness which it induced.

Since the foundation of the government the South had been a minority in the Union, but this weakness seemed of little importance until the great sectional issues arose. The great Calhoun had turned all the resources of his mind to the problem of protecting the minority against the potential tyranny of the majority, and had failed to find a practical solution. There was no solution; but southern statesmen erected one defense after another— constitutional limitations on federal power, political alliances, equal representation in the Senate. All failed. They fell back upon the sovereignty of the state, a doctrine which had been asserted at some time in every section of the Union. It was the last refuge short of secession and acquired the authority of a religious dogma. But as the tide of population rolled westward into new lands that could never be southern, while certain of the border slave states showed a declining interest in slaveholding, it became a question whether the sacred principle of state sovereignty could long withstand the pressure of numbers. What would happen when enough free states had been carved out of the West to give the anti-southern forces three-fourths of all the states in the Union—enough to override the last defenses of the South by constitutional amendments? The desperate tactics of the southern politicians after 1850—the demand for unhampered entry of slave property into western territories where climatic conditions effectively barred the institution, the repeal of the Missouri Compromise, which could give no possible practical advantage to their section—however futile they may seem now, were all fundamentally measures of defense. Their effect was to bring into existence immediately the first great sectional party, the Republican, a party which in some form was certain to emerge sooner or later. The "Black Republicans" (a term which sufficiently distinguished them from Jefferson's organization), whose cardinal principle was opposition to the extension of slavery, professed to harbor no designs against the institution in the states; but they called the abolitionists to their support and counted scores of them among their leaders. Southern men refused to be taken in by platform professions. They knew that Black Republicanism was their implacable enemy.

In October, 1859, John Brown's attempt to head a slave insurrection in Virginia, followed by the northern panegyries lavished upon that "martyred" incendiary, aroused apprehension and indignation throughout the South. Doubtless many of the secessionists secretly rejoiced that the final issue was brought closer; but the majority of the southern people were troubled by the portent of danger. Would they be safe if the antislavery men should win control of the government at the new election? A year later the election of Lincoln and the refusal of the victorious Republicans to agree to any compromise or satisfactory guaranty of their safety convinced them that the time had come for separation and the establishment of a new southern union. In mingled anger, regret, and enthusiasm the cotton states withdrew and set up their Confederacy. The upper South held back until Lincoln's call for troops; then four more states joined to resist the armed invasion from the North.

If the southern people erred grievously in their decision, grievously they answered for it. For four long, weary years they fought an unequal and inherently hopeless struggle for independence, enduring what no civilized people had suffered since Louis XIV ravaged the Palatinate. In the end they were conquered, their slaves freed and their social system overturned, their lands laid waste and left almost worthless, their mills, factories and railroads destroyed or weakened beyond immediate repair, their banks and accumulated credits wiped out, their families impoverished, the flower of their youth dead or crippled. Their conquerors imposed upon this stricken people, in the form of taxes and the repudiation of their bonds, an indemnity heavier than that levied upon France by Imperial Germany in 1871. They faced their condition courageously and sought to build anew upon their broken foundations; but the triumphant North fell under the direction of vindictive leaders who utilized to the utmost the prevailing war psychosis to frustrate every effort of the southern whites to recover something from the general wreck. The orgy of radical reconstruction kindled a new re-

sentment more enduring than that caused by the war itself.

By all odds the bitterest draught held to the lips of the southern whites during reconstruction was their enforced subjection to the political control of their former slaves. Not even the imposition of exorbitant taxes and the plundering of the public treasuries by the carpetbaggers equalled in their eyes this iniquitous humiliation. The purpose of the northern radicals was not so much to uplift the Negro as to "nationalize" the sectional Republican party and thus perpetuate their own control of the government. The Negroes, of course, were not to blame. They had not sought this power; but their ignorance and credulity, their naive delight in their new importance made them easy tools in the hands of unscrupulous leaders. It was impossible to eliminate the venal carpetbagger without depriving the Negro of his political power; and in the process racial antipathies developed which were to be a source of trouble for years to come. There can be no doubt that violence and cruelty toward Negroes was greater after the freedmen were first given the ballot in 1867 than it ever was under slavery; but it is significant that the lower class of whites—those nearest the Negro's social and economic level—were the most active in these disturbances. As the Negro was gradually retired from politics, racial friction decreased, and an increasing number of southern leaders took the enlightened position that in order to make him a useful citizen, the freedman must be encouraged to acquire an education and property. Despite sporadic outbreaks, millions of whites and blacks were able to work together on friendly terms, provided the Negro accept the rôle of dependent. In fact, the average Negro was always glad to attach himself to some white man to whom, as patron and protector, he could turn as a ready source of help in time of trouble. The patron acknowledged the obligation but, however kind to his dependent, never wavered in his determination that the South should remain "a white man's country."

Inevitably, perhaps, this solution of the problem of race relationships found little acceptance in the North where the war had engendered a persistent suspicion of southern motives and where radical Republican "bloody shirt" orators and editors sought to hold their party lines intact by charging southern Democrats with being "as rebellious as in 1861" and with practicing every sort of cruelty upon the "Union-loving freedmen, the wards of the nation." The effect of all this was further to inflame the southern mind and to impede the efforts of enlightened and farseeing men to improve the condition of the Negro as an essential step in the regeneration of the South, since to the less thoughtful majority every plea for the freedman was linked up with the anti-southern propaganda of the hated northern radicals. Again the defense mechanism was set in operation and popular rationalizations about the dangers of "social equality" retarded the solution of the problem of racial adjustments.

Northern publicists continued as they had begun in 1861 to explain the war as "the spawn of those twin devils, treason and slavery." For forty years this theory was elaborated and reiterated until it became accepted in the North as one of the historical verities. Thus the burden which the conqueror always manages to lay upon the spirits of the conquered—the heavy burden of sole responsibility for so much suffering—was loaded upon the southern people. To make it more irritating, southern parents saw school histories put into the hands of their children which discredited their own motives in the desperate struggle they had made to protect their land from invasion and devastation and stigmatized them for rebelling against the moral and philanthropic designs of the

righteous North. Defenders of the southern cause were numerous, but they could get little hearing. Southern political leaders, after they had been allowed to return to Congress, could ill afford, for the sake of their northern Democratic allies, to arouse northern susceptibilities by attempting the vindication of the movement for southern independence. Few were inclined to reargue the cause of slavery, now that it was gone; most men, in fact, expressed satisfaction that it was no more. But none were willing to stultify themselves by admitting that their motives had been bad in 1861. While those who remained "unreconstructed" proclaimed with Robert Toombs that they "had nothing to regret but the dead and the failure," the majority turned hopefully to the future and sought to find compensation for their children in the new South which was somehow to rise miraculously from the ashes of the old.

It was expected that recovery would come through agriculture, for cotton brought an abnormally high price at the end of the war. A few good crops would bring large returns and upon this basis other industries could rebuild. The result was disappointing, for cotton growing recovered only slowly during the turmoil of reconstruction. Throughout wide areas where the federal armies had penetrated, houses, barns, gins and fences had been burned, the stock killed or driven away. The land remained, but its market value was less than half that of 1860 and it often had to be mortgaged in order to procure the means for starting anew. Even the districts which had escaped ravage were in a sad state—tools worn out or broken, stock depleted, neither money nor credit procurable except on ruinous terms. Some of the small cotton crop of 1864 remained in the country, but most of it was seized by rapacious federal agents. The acreage planted in 1865 was small and the harvest generally was poor. The government exacted a tax of three cents per pound on ginned cotton. The labor of rebuilding houses, barns, gins, and fences took time and the cost absorbed the small profits as fast as they came. Although the Negroes, after the first year or so, worked better than was expected, they were kept in a continual state of unrest by carpetbag politicians and soon demanded separate fields as tenants in order to be freer of control. In fact, their former masters were usually unable to pay them monthly wages and could offer them only a share of the crop. The result was that the large plantations were divided into smaller tracts, each worked by a Negro cropper on shares, or else were broken up and sold to small white farmers. The slipshod methods of the cropper reduced the output per acre to less than before the war, so that it was not until 1878, thirteen years after Appomattox, that the cotton crop east of the Mississippi equaled that of 1860. By that time prices were again low; and as the yield increased thereafter they declined still further and profits vanished.

When the planter became the landlord of Negro croppers he must furnish them with teams, tools, food, clothing, and shelter while they made the crop. As he seldom had sufficient cash to provide these things, he must turn to the local merchant for credit, pledging his share of the crop as security. Because of the uncertain quality of the security, he could no longer depend upon the distant factor who had been his creditor before the war. The small farmer, also, must buy on credit from the merchant and give a lien upon his crop. The merchant in turn obtained advances from the wholesaler or jobber, and the chain of credit ran back to the northern manufacturer and his banker. The rate of interest upon the credits advanced on the crop, usually concealed in the high prices of the goods sold, ran from twenty-five to seventy-five per cent. No ordinary business could endure such a drain; and as the prices of farm products fell, farm owners found themselves hopelessly mired in debt. To attempt diversification of the crop

was useless, for the merchant required a large acreage in a "cash crop"—cotton or tobacco—to cover advances of credits or overhanging debts. Hopelessly entangled, thousands of once independent farmers either sold their land or lost it by foreclosure and passed into the status of tenants, or else moved west to Texas to start over again. Farms and plantations were bought up by merchants who then supplied credit directly to their own tenants. Some of the planters moved to town to become merchants themselves. Economic power and prestige passed rapidly from the owner and tiller of the soil to the merchant, banker, and professional man of the town.

As agriculture sank under its burdens, industrialism swept on to increasing power in national affairs. While the southern statesmen, the ablest of the agrarian leaders, were absent from Congress for some fifteen years, the masters of industry had improved their opportunities by obtaining new favors from Congress and by entrenching themselves in the Constitution. They had obtained higher and higher tariffs; they had procured a new national banking system which greatly extended the power of capital over the terms of credit; they had increased the burdens of debtors and the holdings of creditors through the manipulation of federal finances; and they had inserted a "joker" in the fourteenth amendment which effectually prevented the states from controlling the great corporations which did business within their borders. The Republican party, more and more dominated by the eastern wing, was now the servant of big business; and a large section of the eastern wing of the Democratic party, to which the now "solid South" clung with pathetic faith, was committed to the same political-industrial program. The agriculturalists, the cotton and tobacco growers of the South and the grain growers of the West, divided by the bloody chasm of the war, could not make successful resistance.

This condition could not endure without revolt; but successful revolt was made difficult by the peculiar status of southern politics. The grim ten year struggle of the reconstruction period had centered about the question whether the southern whites would be able to recapture control of their local governments. Under the pressure of the northern radicals and the local carpetbaggers and Negroes, southern ante-bellum party lines were obliterated and the mass of southern farmers, planters, business and professional men fused into one party, the Democratic. The "solid South" for which Calhoun had worked in vain had arrived—far more compact than at the time of secession. Apprehension of further federal interference in local affairs, especially in behalf of Negro activities in politics, was a powerful cementing force; and for fifteen years more the political leaders who had cleansed their states of the carpetbag governments continued to guide and rule. They were generally men of high character and great popularity, and the widely conceded necessity of maintaining Democratic solidarity seemed to make their position impregnable. But these leaders, largely of the old planting and professional classes or former officers of the Confederate army, were being drawn into ever closer relations with the new business enterprise which was stirring in the South. Conservative because of tradition and business association, convinced believers in the doctrines of *laissez faire,* they saw only danger in governmental interference with private business. And this at a time when symptoms of revolt were sweeping through the masses of impoverished farmers and tenants—revolt against the unseen forces which depressed the prices of agricultural products and increased debts, against the exactions of the money lender and the extortions of the railroads.

The first agrarian revolt came not in the South, however, but among the farmers of the West who organized the "Patrons of Husbandry" or Grange in the late sixties to provide for better agricultural education, to curb the railroads and monopolies, and to devise a scheme for co-operative buying and selling. The order spread into the cotton country during the next decade, but it collapsed before the southern farmers, still struggling with the fag end of reconstruction, awoke to its possibilities. In the late eighties another organization with a similar purpose, the Farmers' Alliance which began in Texas, made better headway in the South; but internal dissensions, fomented in part by the apprehensive business element, dissipated and destroyed it. Both of these organizations had endeavored to avoid partisan politics in order to prevent divisions within their ranks; but when the farmers found that their old political leaders had nothing to offer them, their discontent broke over into political action. In the South it took the form at first of an uprising against the Bourbon leadership within the Democratic party. In 1890 came the Tillman revolution in South Carolina against the silk stocking aristocracy of the towns. James S. Hogg fought his way to the governorship of Texas with a mandate to curb the insolence of the railway barons. The farmers of Georgia staged a revolt against the triumvirate of Gordon, Colquitt, and Joe Brown. The Bourbons everywhere were suddenly on the defensive. In 1892 the People's Party, forming with startling swiftness, attempted to restore the power of the farmer in both state and national affairs. The southern Populists recalled the Negro to the polls, an evidence of their desperation which startled the conservatives and soon led to more stringent restrictions upon the Negroes' use of the ballot. But the Populist movement broke against the solid wall of party regularity and eventually disappeared, leaving behind it a program which was later adopted, in part, by the old parties after it was seen to be harmless. The Democratic party was itself captured by the advocates of free silver coinage, who thought by increasing the supply of money to get better prices for agricultural products and thus lift the burden of their debts. It was the misfortune of the debt-ridden farmer in his fight against the strangling hold of the capitalist creditor to be forced always to the support of "unsound" economic theories or of "unconstitutional" legislation. When he took up the weapons of his antagonist—cooperation and combination, as in the Grange, the Farmers' Alliance, and the Farmers' Union—his own individualism helped to break the organization down.

Defeat, poverty, frustration, the wearying sense of being eternally on the defensive had their inevitable depressing effects upon social and cultural conditions. The tone of southern life was lower than before the war. The old planter aristocracy, which before 1861 had set the standards of polite society, was broken, scattered, and losing its leadership. It has been the fashion of writers of the forward-looking school to count this as a blessing second only to the destruction of slavery; but before accepting this dictum it may be worth while to inquire what this social order was. While it must be acknowledged that the popular legend of the ante-bellum southern aristocracy contains many absurdities, no one who has honestly tried to understand the group can escape the conclusion that it had qualities which neither the South nor the nation can well afford to lose. It was not necessarily a class of great wealth, even as wealth was counted in those days, but of enough means to afford travel, the possession of books, and the leisure to read them. Its essential character was in its way of life and its attitude toward life; and these, the result of generations of good breeding and quiet living, were rooted deep in traditions of family honor, public responsibility, self-respect, a contempt for lying and cowardice—in short they were the standards of gentlemen and gentlewomen in every age and country. Not all the aristocracy, of course, lived up to the ideals of their class, but the finer representatives of the group exercised an influence on southern life far out of proportion to their numbers. Submerged by the social and economic revolution which followed the war and by the gradual rise to leadership of new groups with "go-getting" ideals, they did not lose their identity nor wholly change their ways of life, for family tradition is strong in the South, but they no longer determined the standards of social conduct.

Personal and sectional poverty, the realization that the South no longer shared in the direction of national affairs, everything that emphasized the painful contrast with the past, caused many of the older generation to look back wistfully to the good old days when the South had an integral and important place in the life of the nation. It was easy to slip into an idealization of the old South, to tinge its receding memories with a roseate glow, to picture it as composed principally of the fine old aristocracy whose homes were ever filled with light and laughter and whose prosperous fields were tilled only by happy, loyal and contented slaves. There was enough substance in the tradition to give it value, and it was seized upon by social climbers, especially by women eager for social prestige and by those shallow nuisances, the professional southerners. Partly from motives which were wholly justified and partly as a defense reaction to northern misrepresentation, the Lost Cause was becoming glorified. Justly proud of the records of their desperate valor survivors of the Confederate armies organized to perpetuate the memories of the War between the States and to commemorate their dead. Hence arose those pathetic monuments which adorn courthouse and capitol lawns throughout the South. And for thirty years an almost indispensable qualification for public office from Virginia to Texas was a good record as a Confederate soldier. . . .

When the opening of the twentieth century brought an end to the long depression int which the whole civilized world had sunk during the eighteen nineties, the agricultural South shared in the upward turn. Better prices for crops, especially for cotton, enabled thousands of those farmers who tilled their own lands to get out of debt. Among this class farming methods improved. The efforts of the agricultural colleges, the farm journals and the expert demonstrators of the new experiment stations began to show results in greater diversification of crops, more interest in the conservation of the soil and more attention to improved breeds of farm stock. New labor-saving machinery enabled the farmer to cultivate more acres and thus to increase his output, while the advent of the automobile shortened the road to market and often enabled his children to attend in some neighboring town a better school than the rural community afforded. But his savings were never large, for as he improved his previously low standards of living his small profits were consumed by the increased cost of everything he had to buy. Paradoxically, the rise in the value of farm products was reflected more in the greater prosperity of the merchant and professional classes of the towns than in that of the farmer himself. And notwithstanding the evident improvement in his condition, the home-owning farmer was being slowly but steadily replaced by the tenant. More and more farm property was passing into the hands of the merchants and professional men of the towns.

In 1900 about forty-five per cent of the farms in the cotton states were worked by tenants; by 1910 the percentage had increased to fifty. The tenants shared little in the benefits of the agricultural revival. For the most part untrained in the better methods of farming, moving frequently from one place to another, intent only upon the existing crop, they had no interest in the conservation of the soil, which deteriorated rapidly under their cultivation. Without capital with which to finance the growing of a crop, they still had to be "furnished" by the merchant at exorbitant credit prices, or by the landlord, mortgaging their cotton before it was planted. Diversification was impossible without capital for purchasing tools and live-stock and without the consent of both landlord and merchant, who usually insisted upon a large acreage in cotton, the cash crop. The standard of living of both black and white tenants was pitiably low. It is not surprising that the more energetic and ambitious children of the independent farmer as well as of the tenant sought escape from the farm to the more attractive life of the towns. Constantly drained of its best element, with tenantry steadily increasing—by 1920 it had risen to fifty-five per cent—the farm population of the cotton states settled dangerously toward the condition of the poorer sort of European peasantry.

Still bound to a colonial economy and a strangling credit system, more than half of the tillers of the soil in these states remain balanced precariously on the edge of bare subsistence. In comparison with the town dwellers, most of the white farmers are in a far worse position than their great-grandfathers were in 1860. This agricultural section is certainly not the new South, rising unshackled by the destruction of slavery, its energies released, regenerated and properous, which Henry Grady visioned some fifty years ago. But however depressed the condition of southern agriculture, there *is* a new South that fulfils in large part Grady's eloquent prophecies. It is the urban South, the product of new industries and commerce.

Perhaps the first authentic sign of the economic recovery of the South after Appomattox was the establishment of new industries and the gradual restoration of others which had collapsed with the Confederacy. Out of the ruck of small log-house tobacco manufacturers in the piedmont of North Carolina emerged a few men of foresight and daring, such as James B. Duke and R. J. Reynolds, who began new ventures and consolidations that grew into giant corporations. In the hill country of northern Alabama and adjacent parts of Georgia and Tennessee small coal and iron mines and iron furnaces had been established before the Civil War. The richest deposits, in northern Alabama, were long inaccessible; but in the early seventies a few enthusiasts began a fight for a railroad to the "Red Mountain." When it had been built, Birmingham arose to become the industrial capital of an enormous coal, iron, and steel district. Consolidation followed consolidation until, in 1907, control of the major part of the coal and steel industry passed into the hands of the United States Steel Corporation. In the meantime the great coal and iron deposits of West Virginia, an extension of the Pennsylvania-Ohio region, were being exploited. Throughout the southern Appalachians the empire of iron and steel extended its dominion. Along the piedmont of the Carolinas and Georgia small cotton mills arose to replace those which had been destroyed or left bankrupt at the close of the war. For many years they developed slowly, for their promoters had to rely upon local capital and to fight the jealous and powerful New England interests; but with the advantage of cheap labor and new machinery they gradually took over the major production of all except the finer grades of cloth. The spirit of William Gregg must have rejoiced when the supremacy finally passed from New England to the southern mill region.

Meanwhile the dismantled southern railroads were slowly rebuilt, usually by means of northern credit and often at the price of northern control. The lines in the border states, especially in Kentucky and Tennessee, which had suffered least or which had been repaired for military use by the Union armies, pushed down into the cotton country or acquired bankrupt roads for connection with the Gulf ports. The Louisville and Nashville and the Illinois Central extended to New Orleans. By 1883 new lines stretched from St. Louis into Texas, to Houston, Galveston, and San Antonio. In the same year New Orleans was connected with San Francisco by the Southern Pacific. J. P. Morgan took over for reorganization a group of Virginia roads which in 1894 became the Southern Railway. Through these extensions and combinations the rising factory towns of the Carolina piedmont acquired direct connection with Baltimore, Philadelphia, and New York, while the lower Mississippi Valley and central Texas were suddenly faced about toward Cincinnati, Chicago, and St. Louis.

While southern agriculture staggered under its burdens, a new urban South was rising to prosperity. The railways had set the currents of trade flowing in new directions and in ever greater volume. Inland towns situated at strategic points, like Atlanta, Memphis and Dallas, obtained advantages in competitive rates and became distributing centers for large territories. To them came new business enterprises—railway shops, machine shops, wholesale houses, department stores, banks, hotels, insurance firms, scores of small shop keepers and retail merchants. The growing population, recruited both from the North and the countryside, was slowly acquiring a cosmopolitan character which was in time to modify profoundly southern traditions and social life.

As compared with the growth of the great northern cities that of the southern towns was not impressive, but it was full of significance for the future of the South. Atlanta's population increased from 37,000 in 1880 to 90,000 in 1900; Memphis rose in the same period from 33,000 to 102,000; Dallas from 10,000 to 42,000. The seaports showed a smaller relative growth than the railroad centers of the interior, for in the same twenty years the population of New Orleans rose from 216,000 to 287,000, while Mobile' grew from 29,000 to only 38,000 and Charles ton's from 50,000 to a bare 56,000. During the succeeding twenty years, a more prosperous period for business, the southern cities grew apace. Richmond doubled its size, rising from 85,000 in 1900 to 171,000 in 1920; Atlanta rose from 90,000 to 200,000; Birmingham shot up from 38,000 to 178,000; New Orleans from 287,000 to 387,000; Dallas from 42,000 to 159,000; Houston grew from 44,000 to 138,000, and San Antonio from 53,000 to 161,000. These figures are only for the incorporated areas; in most instances separately incorporated suburbs swelled the true total by many thousands more. Automobiles and improved highways greatly extended the retail trade of the larger towns at the expense of the smaller neighboring villages; they created a vast new business, stimulated travel and quickened the tempo of life everywhere.

The increase of wealth, as of population, was chiefly in the cities. As taxable values mounted, paved streets, playgrounds and parks multiplied. The urban school systems were enlarged and improved until in buildings, equipment, and curricula they were on a par with those of northern cities. The tax returns from city property enabled the state legislatures, still controlled by the rural districts, to spread a portion of the state revenues over the rural schools. Automobiles and good roads made it possible for many small country schools to consolidate, build better school houses and employ better teachers. Unfortunately, this development was very uneven, for in many states the rural schools were still shabbily housed, ran for short terms and paid low salaries to teachers.

The course of politics reflected the confusion of a transition period. After the Populist uprising of the nineties had subsided, the Democratic organizations resumed their accustomed control of state affairs; but the Democrats seldom had a definite party policy with respect to local matters and, in the absence of a strong opposing party, fell into divisions between rival aspirants for leadership and power. Nevertheless, a considerable public opinion was forming in behalf of more activity by the state governments in promoting the general social welfare. Prior to 1900 the poverty of the people had kept state revenues and expenditures low and had restricted the functions of the governments to the barest essentials; but now improved economic conditions strengthened the demands of the more progressive element for increased expenditures for public improvements, for public education, and for new agencies for social betterment. This program found its chief obstacle in the unreformed tax systems which still laid the heaviest burden upon real estate. The landowners opposed any increase in this tax, while the business corporations resisted every effort to shift a proportionate share of the burden to other forms of wealth. Likewise, a growing demand for the closer regulation of corporate enterprise, especially with respect to labor policies, met the resistance not only of the corporations affected but of other persons who thought that the development of the South depended upon concessions to capitalistic enterprise and of those conservatives who dreaded to see government interfere with the freedom of business. Improvement in these matters, therefore, went forward unevenly, in some states very slowly. The growth of corporate wealth and the opening of new business opportunities lured the ablest men away from public service, so that the average of political leadership was mediocre. In some states it sank even lower, for this was the period which produced Vardaman, Bilbo, and Blease. Outside the mountain sections, where the Republicans had been strong ever since the close of the Civil War, the Democratic party was apparently as strong as ever; but as big business became more and more powerful and drew more interests to its support, the protective tariff found new adherents and thousands of southern business men ventured openly to express admiration for the attitude of the Republican party toward corporate interests. While they might continue to vote with the Democrats, they prayed for Republican success in the national elections.

The South was being swept into national currents. The war with Spain carried thousands of the sons of Confederate veterans into the army and aroused an enthusiasm for "the flag" which caused the United States Congress, dominated by Republicans, to remove the last political restrictions upon ex-Confederates. The growth of cities and the shifting of residence, so characteristic of American business life, tended strongly to break down provincial prejudices. The election of Woodrow Wilson to the presidency brought southern political leaders again to the front in national affairs and made the South, for the first time in over fifty years, feel that it was an integral part of the nation. The World War wiped out most of the bitter memories of the Civil War. To hundreds of thousands of school children today that war is as remote as the Revolution against Great Britain.

In similar fashion, for an increasing number of sourthern people, especially for the younger generation, the traditional culture patterns were breaking down. The greater ease of travel and the constant shifting of business and professional people between northern and southern cities tended to weaken old associations and to set up new standards and attitudes. Thousands of young men and women of the well-to-do urban classes attended northern schools and colleges and made new contacts and friendships. The beginning renascence of southern colleges brought in as instructors scores of young scholars trained in the great graduate schools of northern universities. Some of them, at least, managed to teach the value of scientific methods of investigating not only the physical and biological world, but also the prevailing economic order, the contemporary social organization, and even religious conceptions. Though not always perfectly free to pursue their enquiries far into these mysteries, they called attention to the need for a re-examination of old social values and raised questions which challenged the entire range of traditional concepts and practices. Through books, essays, and uplift magazines the world-wide ferment of discussion spread into the South. . . .

Although new forces are sweeping through the South with the expansion of industries and commerce and the growth of cities, they have as yet touched lightly the rural population. Tenantry, cotton, and the credit system still hold in thralldom the greater portion of the farming class from the Carolinas to Texas. But as year by year the cities grow while the rural communities remain stationary, the center of gravity shifts steadily toward that urban civilization which seems destined to dominate and standardize American life everywhere. Slowly perhaps, but inevitably, as economic and social changes press them into new paths, the southern people will give up those peculiar attitudes which have grown out of their social inheritance and political experience. Whatever the future of American life, they will share it.

Ramsdell concluded with an acknowledgment that the South is gradually moving away from its agricultural traditions and toward an industrial and urban civilization. Acceptance of this inevitable development was not shared by the twelve southerners who wrote *I'll Take My Stand: The South and the Agrarian Tradition* (1930). While this group was not able to halt industrialization, their volume endures as a reminder that southerners have nourished an image of themselves and their region which places much emphasis upon human dignity, grace, leisure, and spiritual and esthetic experiences. This selection is composed of excerpts from chapters written by FRANK L. OWSLEY (1890–1956) and by JOHN CROWE RANSOM (b. 1888). A native of Alabama, Owsley taught history in the state of his birth and at Vanderbilt University for nearly forty years. Called a "modern fire-eater" by some critics, he made no apologies for his sectional allegiance, but his books on the Civil War and the South attest to his scholarship as well as his regional loyalty. Also associated with Vanderbilt University for many years and the acknowledged senior member of the Southern agrarians, Ransom is known as a poet, literary critic, and commentator on American society. Not a static thinker, Ransom, in an essay-review in 1945, stated that the values of civilization will not necessarily be preserved best in an agrarian setting.*

Frank L. Owsley, John Crowe Ransom

The Ideal of an Agrarian Society

Frank L. Owsley, "The Irrepressible Conflict"

Complex though the factors were which finally caused [the Civil] [W]ar, they all grew out of two fundamental differences which existed between the two sections: the North was commercial and industrial, and the South was agrarian. The fundamental and passionate ideal for which the South stood and fell was the ideal of an agrarian society. All else, good and bad, revolved around this ideal—the old and accepted manner of life for which Egypt, Greece, Rome, England, and France had stood. History and literature, profane and sacred, twined their tendrils about the cottage and the villa, not the factory.

When America was settled, the tradition of the soil found hospitable root-bed in the Southern colonies, where climate and land

*From Frank L. Owsley, "The Irrepressible Conflict," pp. 69–74, 90–91, and John Crowe Ransom, "Reconstructed But Unregenerate," pp. 15–22, reprinted from *I'll Take My Stand: The South and the Agrarian Tradition* by Twelve Southerners. Copyright 1930 by Harper & Brothers; renewed 1958 by Donald Davidson. Reprinted by permission of Harper & Row, Publishers.

combined to multiply the richness of an agrarian economy. All who came to Virginia, Maryland, the Carolinas and Georgia were not gentlemen; in fact, only a few were of the gentry. Most of them were of the yeomanry, and they were from rural England with centuries of country and farm lore and folk memory. . . . The environment all pointed toward an endless enjoyment of the fruits of the soil. Jefferson, not visualizing the industrial revolution which whipped up the multiplication of populations and tore their roots from the soil, dreamed of America, free from England, as a boundless Utopia of farms taking a thousand generations to fill.

Men so loved their life upon the soil that they sought out in literature and history peoples who had lived a similar life, so that they might justify and further stimulate their own concepts of life and perhaps set a high goal for themselves among the great nations which had sprung from the land. The people whom they loved most in the ancient world were the Greeks and the Romans of the early republic. The Greeks did not appeal to them as did the Romans, for they were too inclined to neglect their farms and turn to the sea and to handicraft. But the even-poised and leisurely life of the Greeks, their oratory, their philosophy, their art—especially their architecture—appealed to the South. The Greek tradition became partly grafted upon the Anglo-Saxon and Scotch tradition of life. However, it was the Romans of the early republic . . . who appealed most powerfully to the South. These Romans were brave, sometimes crude, but open and without guile—unlike the Greeks. They reeked of the soil, of the plow and the spade; they had wrestled with virgin soil and forests; they could build log houses and were closer to many Southerners than even the English gentleman in his moss-covered stone house. It was Cincinnatus, whose hands were rough with guiding the plow, rather than Cato, who wrote about Roman agriculture and lived in a villa, whom Southerners admired the most, though they read and admired Cato as a fine gentleman with liberal ideas about tenants and slaves and a thorough knowledge and love of the soil. The Gracchi appealed to Southerners because the Gracchi were lovers of the soil and died in the attempt to restore the yeomanry to the land.

With the environment of the New World and the traditions of the Old, the South thus became the seat of an agrarian civilization which had strength and promise for a future greatness second to none. The life of the South was leisurely and unhurried for the planter, the yeoman, or the landless tenant. It was a way of life, not a routine of planting and reaping merely for gain. Washington, who rode daily over his farms and counted his horses, cattle, plows, and bushels of corn as carefully as a merchant takes stock of his supplies, inhaled the smell of ripe corn after a rain, nursed his bluegrass sod and shade trees with his own hands, and, when in the field as a soldier or in the city as President of the United States, was homesick at the smell of fresh-plowed earth. He kept vigil with his sick horses and dogs, not as a capitalist who guards his investments, but as one who watches over his friends.

The system of society which developed in the South, then, was close to the soil. It might be organized about the plantation with its wide fields and its slaves and self-sufficiency, or it might center around a small farm, ranging from a fifty-acre to a five-hundred-acre tract, tilled by the owner, undriven by competition, supplied with corn by his own toil and with meat from his own pen or from the fields and forests. The amusements might be the fine balls and house parties of the planter or the three-day break-down dances which David Crockett loved, or horse races, foot races, cock and dog fights, boxing, wrestling, shooting, fighting, logrolling, house raising, or corn-shucking. It might be crude or genteel, but it everywhere was fundamentally alike and natural. The houses were homes, where families lived sufficient and complete within themselves, working together and fighting together. And when death came, they were buried in their own lonely peaceful graveyards, to await doomsday together.

This agrarian society had its own interests, which in almost all respects diverged from the interests of the industrial system of the North. The two sections, North and South, had entered the revolution against the mother country with the full knowledge of the opposing interests of their societies; knowing this difference, they had combined in a loose union under the Articles of Confederation. Finally, they had joined together under the Constitution fully conscious that there were thus united two divergent economic and social systems, two civilizations, in fact. The two sections were evenly balanced in population and in the number of states, so that at the time there was no danger of either section's encroaching upon the interests of the other. This balance was clearly understood. Without it a union would not have been possible. Even with the understanding that the two sections would continue to hold this even balance, the sections were very careful to define and limit the powers of the federal government lest one section with its peculiar interests should get control of the national government and use the powers of that government to exploit the other section. Specific powers were granted the federal government, and all not specifically granted were retained by the states.

But equilibrium was impossible under expansion and growth. One section with its peculiar system of society would at one time or another become dominant and control the national government and either exploit the other section or else fail to exercise the functions of government for its positive benefit. Herein lies the irrepressible conflict, the eternal struggle between the agrarian South

and the commercial and industrial North to control the government either in its own interest or, negatively, to prevent the other section from controlling it in its interests. Lincoln and Seward and the radical Republicans clothed the conflict later in robes of morality by making it appear that the "house divided against itself" and the irrepressible conflict which resulted from this division marked a division between slavery and freedom.

Slavery . . . was part of the agrarian system, but only one element and not an essential one. To say that the irrepressible conflict was between slavery and freedom is . . . to fail to grasp the nature and magnitude of the conflict. . . .

The irrepressible conflict . . . was not between slavery and feeedom, but between the industrial and commercial civilization of the North and the agrarian civilization of the South. . . .

Thus the two sections clashed . . . . Their economic systems and interests conflicted. Their social systems were hostile; their political philosophies growing out of their economic and social systems were as impossible to reconcile as it is to cause two particles of matter to occupy the same space at the same time; and their philosophies of life, growing out of the whole situation in each section, were as two elements in deadly combat. What was food for the one was poison for the other. . . .

This struggle between an agrarian and an industrial civilization, then, was the irrepressible conflict, the house divided against itself. . . .

John Crowe Ransom,
"Reconstructed But Unregenerate"

The North and the South fought, and the consequences were disastrous to both. The Northern temper was one of jubilation and expansiveness, and now it was no longer shackled by the weight of the conservative

Southern tradition. Industrialism, the latest form of pioneering and the worst, presently overtook the North, and in due time has now produced our present American civilization. Poverty and pride overtook the South; poverty to bring her institutions into disrepute and to sap continually at her courage; and a false pride to inspire a distaste for the thought of fresh pioneering projects, and to doom her to an increasing physical enfeeblement.

It is only too easy to define the malignant meaning of industrialism. It is the contemporary form of pioneering; yet since it never consents to define its goal, it is a pioneering on principle, and with an accelerating speed. Industrialism is a program under which men, using the latest scientific paraphernalia, sacrifice comfort, leisure, and the enjoyment of life to win Pyrrhic victories from nature at points of no strategic importance. Ruskin and Carlyle feared it nearly a hundred years ago, and now it may be said that their fears have been realized partly in England, and with almost fatal completeness in America. Industrialism is an insidious spirit, full of false promises and generally fatal to establishments since, when it once gets into them for a little renovation, it proposes never again to leave them in peace. Industrialism is rightfully menial, of almost miraculous cunning but no intelligence; it needs to be strongly governed or it will destroy the economy of the household. Only a community of tough conservative habit can master it.

The South did not become industrialized; she did not repair the damage to her old establishment, either, and it was in part because she did not try hard enough. Hers is the case to cite when we would show how the good life depends on an adequate pioneering, and how the pioneering energy must be kept ready for call when the establishment needs overhauling. The Southern tradition came to look rather pitiable in its persistence when the twentieth century had arrived, for the establishment was quite depreciated. Unregen-erate Southerners were trying to live the good life on a shabby equipment, and they were grotesque in their effort to make an art out of living when they were not decently making the living. In the country districts great numbers of these broken-down Southerners are still to be seen in patched blue-jeans, sitting on ancestral fences, shotguns across their laps and hound-dogs at their feet, surveying their unkempt acres while they comment shrewdly on the ways of God. It is their defect that they have driven a too easy, an unmanly bargain with nature, and that their aestheticism is based on insufficient labor.

But there is something heroic, and there may prove to be yet something very valuable to the Union, in their extreme attachment to a certain theory of life. They have kept up a faith which was on the point of perishing from this continent.

Of course it was only after the Civil War that the North and the South came to stand in polar opposition to each other. Immediately after Appomattox it was impossible for the South to resume even that give-and-take of ideas which had marked her ante-bellum relations with the North. She was offered such terms that acquiescence would have been abject. She retired within her borders in rage and held the minimum of commerce with the enemy. Persecution intensified her tradition, and made the South more solid and more Southern in the year 1875, or thereabouts, than ever before. When the oppression was left off, naturally her guard relaxed. But though the period of persecution had not been long, nevertheless the Southern tradition found itself then the less capable of uniting gracefully with the life of the Union; for that life in the meantime had been moving on in an opposite direction. The American progressive principle was like a ball rolling down the hill with an increasing momentum, and by 1890 or 1900 it was clear to any intelligent Southerner that it was a principle of boundless aggression against nature which could hardly offer much to a society devoted to the arts of peace.

But to keep on living shabbily on an insufficient patrimony is to decline, both physically and spiritually. The South declined.

And now the crisis in the South's decline has been reached.

Industrialism has arrived in the South. Already the local chambers of commerce exhibit the formidable data of Southern progress. A considerable party of Southern opinion, which might be called the New South party, is well pleased with the recent industrial accomplishments of the South and anxious for many more. Southerners of another school, who might be said to compose an Old South party, are apprehensive lest the section become completely and uncritically devoted to the industrial ideal precisely as the other sections of the Union are. But reconstruction is actually under way. Tied politically and economically to the Union, her borders wholly violable, the South now sees very well that she can restore her prosperity only within the competition of an industrial system.

After the war the Southern plantations were often broken up into small farms. These have yielded less and less of a living, and it said that they will never yield a good living until once more they are integrated into large units. But these units will be industrial units, controlled by a board of directors or an executive rather than a squire, worked with machinery, and manned not by farmers living at home, but by "labor." Even so they will not, according to Mr. Henry Ford, support the population that wants to live on them. In the off seasons the laborers will have to work in factories, which henceforth are to be counted on as among the charming features of Southern landscape. The Southern problem is complicated, but at its center is the farmer's problem, and this problem is simply the most acute version of that general agrarian problem which inspires the despair of many thoughtful Americans today.

The agrarian discontent in America is deeply grounded in the love of the tiller for the soil, which is probably, it must be confessed, not peculiar to the Southern specimen, but one of the more ineradicable human attachments, be the tiller as progressive as he may. In proposing to wean men from this foolish attachment, industrialism sets itself against the most ancient and the most humane of all the modes of human livelihood. Do . . . the distinguished thinkers at Washington see how essential is the mutual hatred between the industrialists and the farmers, and how mortal is their conflict? The gentlemen at Washington are mostly preaching and legislating to secure the fabulous "blessings" of industrial progress; they are on the industrial side. The industrialists have a doctrine which is monstrous, but they are not monsters personally; they are forward-lookers with nice manners, and no American progressivist is against them. The farmers are boorish and inarticulate by comparison. Progressivism is against them in their fight, though their traditional status is still so strong that soft words are still spoken to them. All the solutions recommended for their difficulties are really enticements held out to them to become a little more cooperative, more mechanical, more mobile—in short, a little more industrialized. But the farmer who is not a mere laborer, even the farmer of the comparatively new places like Iowa and Nebraska, is necessarily among the more stable and less progressive elements of society. He refuses to mobilize himself and become a unit in the industrial army, because he does not approve of army life.

I will use some terms which are hardly in his vernacular. He identifies himself with a spot of ground, and this ground carries a good deal of meaning; it defines itself for him as nature. He would till it not too hurriedly and not too mechanically to observe in it the contingency and the infinitude of nature; and so his life acquires its philosophical and even its cosmic consciousness. A man can contemplate and explore, respect and love, an object as substantial as a farm or a native province. But he cannot contemplate nor explore, respect nor love, a mere turnover, such as an assemblage of "natural resources," a pile of money, a volume of produce, a market, or a credit system. It is into precisely these intangibles that industrialism would translate the farmer's farm. It means the dehumanization of his life.

However that may be, the South at last, looking defensively about her in all directions upon an industrial world, fingers the weapons of industrialism. There is one powerful voice in the South which, tired of a long status of disrepute, would see the South made at once into a section second to none in wealth, as that is statistically reckoned, and in progressiveness, as that might be estimated by the rapidity of the industrial turnover. This desire offends those who would still like to regard the South as, in the old sense, a home; but its expression is loud and insistent. The urban South, with its heavy importation of regular American ways and regular American citizens, has nearly capitulated to these novelties. It is the village South and the rural South which supply the resistance, and it is lucky for them that they represent a vast quantity of inertia.

Will the Southern establishment, the most substantial exhibit on this continent of a society of the European and historic order, be completely crumbled by the powerful acid of the Great Progressive Principle? Will there be no more looking backward but only looking forward? Is our New World to be dedicated forever to the doctrine of newness?

It is in the interest of America as a whole, as well as in the interest of the South, that these questions press for an answer. I will enter here the most important items of the situation as well as I can; doubtless they will appear a little over-sharpened for the sake of exhibition.

(1) The intention of Americans at large appears now to be what it was always in danger of becoming: an intention of being infinitely progressive. But this intention cannot permit of an established order of human existence, and of that leisure which conditions the life of intelligence and the arts.

(2) The old South, if it must be defined in a word, praticed the contrary and European philosophy of establishment as the foundation of the life of the spirit. The ante-bellum Union possessed, to say the least, a wholesome variety of doctrine.

(3) But the South was defeated by the Union on the battlefield with remarkable decisiveness, and the two consequences have been dire: the Southern tradition was physically impaired, and has ever since been unable to offer an attractive example of its philosophy in action; and the American progressive principle has developed into a pure industrialism without any check from a Southern minority whose voice ceased to make itself heard.

(4) The further survival of the Southern tradition as a detached local remnant is now unlikely. It is agreed that the South must make contact again with the Union. And in adapting itself to the actual state of the Union, the Southern tradition will have to consent to a certain industrialization of its own.

(5) The question at issue is whether the South will permit herself to be so industrialized as to lose entirely her historic identity, and to remove the last substantial barrier that has stood in the way of American progressivism; or will accept industrialism, but with a very bad grace, and will manage to maintain a good deal of her traditional philosophy.

DAVID M. POTTER (b. 1910) was born in Georgia, educated in the North, and now lives in the West, where he is Coe Professor of History at Stanford University. He has written *Lincoln and His Party in the Secession Crisis* (1942) and *People of Plenty: Economic Abundance and the American Character* (1954). In the essay below Potter reviews the approach a number of writers have taken concerning the élan of the South, with especial reference to the agrarian theme. Refusing to equate agrarianism with the South, he suggests that the mystery of the South is best explained by that region's distinctive folk culture.*.

David M. Potter

A Persistent Folk Culture

Among the many flourishing branches of American historical study during the last half-century, one of the most robust has been the history of the South. Fifty years ago, there was already one large body of literature on the Southern Confederacy, especially in its military aspects, and another on the local history of various Southern states, but the history of the South as a region—of the whole vast area below the Potomac viewed as a single entity for the whole time from the settlement of Jamestown to the present—is largely a product of the last five decades. Today, a multi-volume history, a number of college textbooks, a quarterly journal, and a substantial library of monographic studies all serve as measures of the extent of the development in this field.

Anyone who seeks an explanation for this interest in Southern history must take account of several factors. To begin with, the study of American regions is a general phenomenon, embracing not only the South but also New England, the Middle West, and the great physiographic provinces beyond the Mississippi. In a nation as vast and as diverse as ours, there is really no level higher than the regional level at which one can come to grips with the concrete realities of the land. But apart from this regional aspect, the Southern theme has held an unusual appeal for the people of the South because of their peculiarly strong and sentimental loyalty to Dixie as their native land, and for Americans outside the South because of the exotic quality of the place and because it bears the aura of a Lost

*David M. Potter, "The Enigma of the South," *The Yale Review*, LI (October, 1961), 142–146, 149–151. Copyright © 1961 by Yale University.

Cause. Union generals, for some reason, have never held the romantic interest that attached to Stonewall Jackson, Jeb Stuart, George Pickett, Bedford Forrest, and of course, Robert E. Lee. Today, the predilection of Yankee children for caps, flags, and toys displaying the Rebel insignia bears further witness to the enduring truth that lost causes have a fascination even for those who did not lose them.

But it seems unlikely that either the South as an American region, or the South as Dixieland, or the South as a Lost Cause could hold so much scholarly and popular attention in focus if the South were not also an enigma. To writers for more than half a century the South has been a kind of Sphinx on the American land. . . . [N]ot long ago the South was regarded by many thoughtful and liberal-minded people as a kind of sanctuary of the American democratic tradition. What is now deplored as the "benighted South," or the "sick South," was, until recently, regarded by many liberals as the birthplace and the natural bulwark of the Jeffersonian ideal—a region where agrarian democracy still struggled to survive, fighting a gallant rear-guard action against the commercialism and the industrial capitalism of the Northeast.

It would be a major undertaking to trace the evolution of this concept. The general idea that American democracy is essentially frontier democracy—which closely resembles agrarian democracy—is forever linked with Frederick Jackson Turner, but Turner gave it a Western rather than a Southern orientation. Certainly one of the earliest writers to apply it to the South was William E. Dodd. In 1911 . . . he wrote a sketchy little book, now largely forgotten, entitled *Statesmen of the Old South,* with the significant subtitle, *From Radicalism to Conservative Revolt.* The statesmen whom he treated were Jefferson, Calhoun, and Jefferson Davis, and the theme which he developed was that the democratic or radical South of Thomas Jef-

ferson—an equalitarian South of small subsistence farmers—had been subverted by the increasingly aristocratic and hierarchical South of the great slaveholders whose property interests found embodiment in Calhoun and Davis.

In three brief and seemingly artless chapters, Dodd achieved two very subtle effects: first, he defined to suit himself what may be called a normative South—the South of Thomas Jefferson—and thus established an arbitrary basis for identifying all future developments of a Jeffersonian tenor as truly or intrinsically Southern, and rejecting all conservative or hierarchical developments as aberrations of Southernism. Using this device, he then proceeded to dispose of the whole conservative, slaveholding South of ante-bellum fame as a kind of deviation or detour in the true course of Southern history. Thus he finessed the basic question whether the true and realistic image of the South might not be a dualism, with as much of Calhoun as of Jefferson in it, or even whether the true South, historically, is not hierarchical and conservative rather than radical and equalitarian.

In justice to Dodd, one must recognize that his version of Southernism was by no means without foundations. Jeffersonianism, as well as Jefferson, did have distinctively Southern origins, and at almost every decisive turning-point in the advancement of American democracy—whether at the time of Jackson, or Bryan, or Wilson, or Franklin Roosevelt—the South has thrown crucial weight on the democratic side. Still, there was something of a tour de force about the way in which Dodd reconciled his love for his native South and his commitment to democracy, and with very little disclosure of the wishful thinking which was involved, identified the land he loved with the values he cherished.

Whether later writers were directly influenced by Dodd or not, the theme of agrarianism has persisted ever since in the literature of the South, sometimes with the most startling implications. Thus when Charles and Mary Beard came to write about the Civil War in their *Rise of American Civilization* (1927), they pictured it as a conflict between Southern agrarianism and Northern industrialism; in this way, the defenders of slavery were transmuted into democrats, more or less, since agrarianism was, in the Beards' lexicon, by definition democratic, and industrialism was antidemocratic. Again, at the hands of the Beards and of the late Howard K. Beale, in his *The Critical Year,* published in 1930, Reconstruction was not primarily a contest over the rights of Negro freedmen, but rather a series of coups by industrial capitalism to consolidate its ascendancy and to retain its wartime gains, consisting of tariffs, subsidies, and a monetary system favorable to creditors. The Fourteenth Amendment was not a Magna Carta of freedmen's rights, but rather a bulwark for property interests, disguised as a Negro rights measure in order to catch votes. Again, the implications were ironic: for instance, under this formula, Andrew Johnson, a onetime slaveowner and an obdurate foe of Negro rights, appeared as a champion of democracy against the predatory capitalists. Thus Johnson received ecstatic praise in a biography (1929) by that archliberal attorney, Lloyd Paul Stryker, who later became a crusading spokesman for Negro rights.

Through all of these treatments there runs a persistent implied affirmation of Dodd's cleverly articulated premise: that which is agrarian in the South is truly Southern; anything not in the agrarian tradition is somehow extraneous —a cowbird's egg in the Southern nest. . . .

. . . the agrarian premise shows itself also in many of the writings of C. Vann Woodward, the foremost historian of the modern South. In Woodward's biography of *Tom Watson* (1938), for instance, the protagonist of the drama is Watson, the agrarian,

and the antagonists are the Bourbon Democrats who have betrayed the interests of the South to the forces of industrial capitalism. Or alternatively, one could say, the protagonist is the earlier Watson, who championed Populism and defended Negro rights, while the antagonist is the later Watson, a reactionary racist who betrayed the ideals of his youth. Though Woodward's treatment is deeply subtle and sensitive to complexities, while Dodd's was superficial and grossly oversimplified, both are alike in regarding the agrarian South as, almost a priori, the true South, and any force within the South which runs counter to it as an aberration. This is, of course, quite a different thing from merely favoring the agrarian cause.

Although a whole generation of writers have made this tempting equation between Southernism and agrarianism, it requires only a limited analysis to see that in many respects, the Southern economy and the Southern society have not been agrarian at all—in fact, have embodied almost the antithesis of agrarianism. Agrarianism implies an escape from the commercialism of the money economy, but Southern cotton and tobacco and sugar cultivators have consistently been agricultural businessmen producing for market and for cash income. Agrarianism implies production for use rather than production for sale, and therefore diversification rather than specialization, but the Southern agriculturist stuck to his one-crop system in the past as tenaciously as he clings to segregation at the present. It implies the independence of a husbandman who looks to no one else either for his access to the land or for the necessities of his living, but the Southern cultivator has been historically either a slave or a share-cropper, without land and often without opportunity even to grow his own turnip greens in a garden patch. Meanwhile the Southern landowner, whether an absentee planter or a mortgage-holding bank, frequently failed to follow the ennobling agrarian practice of laboring in the earth. To one who is impressed by these aspects, it may seem realistic to regard Calhoun rather than Jefferson as the typical leader of the South; the plantation producing raw materials for the textile industry, rather than the subsistence farm producing for use, as the typical economic unit; hierarchy rather than equality as the typical social condition; and conservatism rather than radicalism as the typical mode of thought. . . .

The continued acceleration of industrial growth . . . showed that agrarianism had no future, but it was still widely believed to have a past, and historians continued to apply it to the interpretation of American history. Henry Bamford Parkes made brilliant use of it in his *The American Experience* (1947), and as recently as 1949, Frank L. Owsley, in his *Plain Folk of the Old South,* delineated the structure of ante-bellum society in terms in which large slaveholders and plain farmers were practically indistinguishable. In these and many other writings, a number of time-honored propositions continued to find acceptance: that American democracy has been nourished primarily from agrarian roots; that agrarian attitudes are inherently democratic; and that the South peculiarly embodies the agrarian tradition.

But of late, the first two of these propositions have come under criticism, and the agrarian view has been attacked, for the first time, at its foundations. As long ago as 1945, Arthur Schlesinger, Jr., in his *Age of Jackson,* offered the then-heretical view that Jacksonian democracy owed more to the East and to class-conscious urban workingmen than to the frontier and its coonskin equality. More recently, Richard Hofstadter, in his *Age of Reform* (1955), has gone even further by arguing that Populism had little affinity with liberal democracy, and was in fact a seed-bed for such illiberal manifestations as prohibition, nativism, immigration restriction, Red-baiting, and the like. Thus, according to

Schlesinger, democracy was not agrarian, and according to Hofstadter, agrarianism was not democratic.

In literal form, the agrarian formula fitted the South remarkably badly. It envisioned a subsistence economy, agricultural diversification, a wide distribution of small landholdings, a large class of independent husbandmen, and an unstratified society. The cold fact is that none of these features has ever been dominant in the South. In the light of these flaws, as well as of recent criticisms, the whole idea of the South as an agrarian society now seems more and more an illusion, nourished by a wish. But once it is discarded, the question reverts to the enigma of the South. All theory aside, is the South, at a purely descriptive level, distinguishable? . . .

On the face of it, it seems a matter of observation and not of theory to say that the culture of the folk survived in the South long after it succumbed to the onslaught of urban-industrial culture elsewhere. It was an aspect of this culture that the relation between the land and the people remained more direct and more primal in the South than in other parts of the country. (This may be more true for the Negroes than for the whites, but then there is also a question whether the Negroes may not have embodied the distinctive qualities of the Southern character even more than the whites.) Even in the most exploitative economic situations, this culture retained a personalism in the relations of man to man which the industrial culture lacks. Even for those whose lives were narrowest, it offered a relationship of man to nature in which there was a certain fulfillment of personality. Every culture is, among other things, a system of relationships among an aggregate of people, and as cultures differ, the systems of relationship vary. In the folk culture of the South, it may be that the relation of people to one another imparted a distinctive texture as well as a distinctive tempo to their lives.

An explanation of the South in terms of a

folk culture would not have the ideological implications which have made the explanation in terms of agrarianism so tempting and at the same time so treacherous. But on the other hand, it would not be inconsistent with some of the realities of Southern society, such as bi-racialism and hierarchy, whereas agrarianism is inconsistent with these realities. The enigma remains, and the historian must still ask what distinctive quality it was in the life of the South for which Southerners have felt such a persistent, haunting nostalgia and to which even the Yankee has responded with a poignant impulse. We must now doubt that this nostalgia was the yearning of men for an ideal agrarian utopia which never existed in reality. But if it was not that, was it perhaps the yearning of men in a mass culture for the life of a folk culture which did really exist? This folk culture, we know, was far from being ideal or utopian, and was in fact full of inequality and wrong, but if the nostalgia persists was it because even the inequality and wrong were parts of a life that still had a relatedness and meaning which our more bountiful life in the mass culture seems to lack?

Arkansas-born C. VANN WOODWARD (b. 1908),
formerly professor at The Johns Hopkins University and now
Sterling Professor of History at Yale University, has
significantly deepened our understanding of the South with
Tom Watson: Agrarian Rebel (1938), *Reunion and Reaction*
(1951), *Origins of the New South* (1951), *The Strange
Career of Jim Crow* (1955), *The Burden of Southern History*
(1960), and numerous interpretive essays. In this selection he
addresses himself to the problem of the South's identity.
While some writers believe the South will soon be nothing
more than a geographical expression, Woodward accepts the
fact that recent changes will greatly alter the region, but he
concludes that the South's past—its tragedy, poverty,
frustration, failure, and guilt—will remain as the
distinguishing mark of the region.*

C. Vann Woodward

The Heritage of History

The time is coming, if indeed it has not
already arrived, when the Southerner will
begin to ask himself whether there is really
any longer very much point in calling himself
a Southerner. Or if he does, he might well
wonder occasionally whether it is worth
while insisting upon the point. So long as he
remains at home where everybody knows him
the matter hardly becomes an issue. But when
he ventures among strangers, particularly up
North, how often does he yield to the impulse
to suppress the identifying idiom, to avoid the
awkward subject, and to blend inconspicu-
ously into the national pattern, to act the role
of the standard American? Has the Southern
heritage become an old hunting jacket that
one slips on comfortably while at home but

discards when he ventures abroad in favor of
some more conventional or modish garb? Or
perhaps an attic full of ancestral wardrobes
useful only in connection with costume balls
and play acting—staged primarily in
Washington, D.C.?. . .

The South is . . . in the midst of an economic and social revolution that has by no
means run its course, and it will not be possible to measure its results for a long time to
come. This revolution has already leveled
many of the old monuments of regional distinctiveness and may end eventually by
erasing the very consciousness of a distinctive
tradition along with the will to sustain it. The
sustaining will and consciousness are also
under the additional strain of a moral in-

*C. Vann Woodward, "The Search for Southern Identity," *The Virginia Quarterly Review,* XXXIV (Summer,
1958), 321–325, 328–338. Reprinted by permission of the author and his publisher.

dictment against a discredited part of the tradition, an indictment more uncompromising than any since abolitionist times.

The Southerner may not have been very happy about many of those old monuments of regional distinctiveness that are now disappearing. He may, in fact, have deplored the existence of some—the one–horse farmer, one–crop agriculture, one–party politics, the sharecropper, the poll tax, the white primary, the Jim Crow car, the lynching bee. It would take a blind sentimentalist to mourn their passing. But until the day before yesterday there they stood, indisputable proof that the South was different. Now that they are vanished or on their way toward vanishing, we are suddenly aware of the vacant place they have left in the landscape and of our habit of depending upon them in final resort as landmarks of regional identification. To establish identity by reference to our faults was always simplest, for whatever their reservations about our virtues, our critics were never reluctant to concede us our vices and faults.

It is not that the present South has any conspicuous lack of faults, but that its faults are growing less conspicuous and therefore less useful for purposes of regional identification. They are increasingly the faults of other parts of the country, standard American faults, shall we say? Many of them have only recently been acquired, could, in fact, only recently be afforded. For the great changes that are altering the cultural landscape of the South almost beyond recognition are not simply negative changes, the disappearance of the familiar. There are also positive changes, the appearance of the strikingly new.

The symbol of innovation is inescapable. The roar and groan and dust of it greet one on the outskirts of every Southern city. That symbol is the bulldozer, and for lack of a better name this might be called the Bulldozer Revolution. The great machine with the lowered blade symbolizes the revolution in

several respects: in its favorite area of operation for one, the area where city meets country; in its relentless speed for another; in its supreme disregard for obstacles, its heedless methods; in what it demolishes and in what it builds. It is the advance agent of the metropolis. It encroaches upon rural life to expand urban life. It demolishes the old to make way for the new.

It is not the amount of change that is impressive about the Bulldozer Revolution so much as the speed and concentration with which it has come, and with which it continues. In the decade of the forties, when urbanization was growing at a swift pace in the country as a whole, the cities of the South's fifty-three metropolitan areas grew more than three times as fast as comparable cities in the rest of the country, at a rate of 33.1 per cent as compared with 10.3 per cent elsewhere. For every three city dwellers in the South at the beginning of that decade there were four at the end and for every five farm residents there were only four. An overwhelmingly rural South in 1930 had 5.5 millions employed in agriculture; by 1950 only 3.2 millions.

According to nearly all of the indices, so the economists find, the economic growth of the South in recent years greatly exceeds the rate maintained in the North and East. The fact is that the South is going through economic expansion and reorganization that the North and East completed a generation or more ago. But the process is taking place far more rapidly in the South than it did in the North. Among all the many periods of change in the history of the South, it is impossible to find one of such concentration and such substantive impact. The period of Reconstruction might appear a likely rival for this distinction, but that revolution was largely limited to changes in legal status and the ownership of property. The people remained pretty much where they were and continued to make their living in much the same way.

All indications are that the bulldozer will leave a deeper mark upon the land than did the carpetbagger.

It is the conclusion of two Southern sociologists that the South's present drive toward uniformity "with national demographic, economic, and cultural norms might well hasten the day when the South, once perhaps the most distinctively 'different' American region, will have become in most such matters virtually indistinguishable from the other urban-industrial areas of the nation."

The threat of becoming "indistinguishable," of being submerged under a national steamroller, has haunted the mind of the South for a long time. Some have seen it as a menace to regional identity and the survival of a Southern heritage. . . .

With the crumbling of so many defenses in the present, the South has tended to substitute myths about the past. Every self-conscious group of any size fabricates myths about its past: about its origins, its mission, its righteousness, its benevolence, its general superiority. But few groups in the New World have had their myths subjected to such destructive analysis as those of the South have undergone in recent years. Southern historians themselves have been the leading iconoclasts and their attacks have spared few of the South's cherished myths.

The Cavalier Legend as the myth of origin was one of the earlier victims. The Plantation Legend of ante-bellum grace and elegance has not been left wholly intact. The pleasant image of a benevolent and paternalistic slavery system as a school for civilizing savages has suffered damage that is probably beyond repair. Even the consoling security of Reconstruction as the common historic grievance, the infallible mystique of unity has been rendered somewhat less secure by detached investigation. And finally, rude hands have been laid upon the hallowed memory of the Redeemers who did in the Carpetbaggers, and doubt has been cast upon the antiquity of segregation folk ways. These faded historical myths are weak material for buttressing Southern defenses, for time has dealt as roughly with them as with agrarianism and racism.

Would a hard won immunity from the myths and illusions of Southern sectionalism provide some immunity to the illusions and myths of American nationalism? Or would the hasty divestment merely make the myth-denuded Southerner hasten to wrap himself in the garments of nationalism? The danger in the wholesale rejection of the South by the modern Southerner bent on reaffirming his Americanism is the danger of affirming more than he bargains for.

While the myths of Southern distinctiveness have been waning, national myths have been waxing in power and appeal. National myths, American myths have proved far more sacrosanct and inviolate than Southern myths. Millions of European people of diverse cultural backgrounds have sought and found identity in them. The powerful urge among minority groups to abandon or disguise their distinguishing cultural traits and conform as quickly as possible to some national norm is one of the most familiar features in the sociology of American nationalism. European ethnic and national groups with traditions far more ancient and distinctive than those of the South have eagerly divested themselves of their cultural heritage in order to conform.

The conformist is not required or expected to abandon his distinctive religion. But whether he remains a Protestant, a Catholic, or a Jew, his religion typically becomes subordinate or secondary to a national faith. Foreign observers have remarked that the different religions in America resemble each other more than they do their European counterparts. "By every realistic criterion," writes Will Herberg in his study of American religious sociology, "the American Way of Life is the operative faith of the American people." And where the mandates of the American Way of Life conflict with others they take undisputed sway over the masses of all religions. Herberg describes it as "a faith that has its symbols and its rituals, its holidays and its liturgy, its saints and its sancta," and it is common to all Americans. "Sociologically, anthropologically, if one pleases," he writes, the American Way of Life "is the characteristic American religion, undergirding American life and overarching American society despite all indubitable differences of region, section, culture, and class." Differences such as those of region and section, "indubitable" though he admits them to be, he characterizes as "peripheral and obsolescent."

If the American Way of Life has become a religion, any deviation from it has become a sort of heresy. Regionalism in the typical American view is rather like the Turnerian frontier, a section on the move—or at least one that should keep moving, and moving in a course that converges at not too remote a point with the American Way. It is a season's halt of the American caravan, a temporary encampment of an advancing society, eternally on the move toward some undefined goal of progress.

The same urge to conformity that operates upon ethnic or national minorities to persuade them to reject identification with their native heritage or that of their forebears operates to a degree upon the Southerner as well. Since the cultural landscape of his native region is being altered almost beyond recognition by a cyclone of social change, the Southerner may come to feel as uprooted as the immigrant. Bereft of his myths, his peculiar institutions, even his familiar regional vices, he may well reject or forget his regional identification as completely as the immigrant.

Is there nothing about the South that is immune from the disintegrating effect of nationalism and the pressure for conformity? Is there not something that has not changed?

There is only one thing that I can think of, and that is its history. By that I do not mean a Southern brand of Shintoism, the worship of ancestors. Nor do I mean written history and its interpretation, popular and mythical, or professional and scholarly, which has changed often and will change again. I mean rather the collective experience of the Southern people. It is in just this respect that the South remains the most distinctive region of the country. In their unique historic experience as Americans the Southerners should not only be able to find the basis for continuity of their heritage, but also make contributions that balance and complement the experience of the rest of the nation.

At this point the risks of our enterprise multiply. They are the risks of spawning new myths in place of the old. Awareness of them demands that we redouble precautions and look more cautiously than ever at generalizations.

To start with a safe one, it can be assumed that one of the most conspicuous traits of American life has been its economic abundance. From early colonial days the fabulous riches of America have been compared with the scarcity and want of less favored lands. Immense differentials in economic welfare and living standards between the United States and other countries still prevail. In an illuminating book called "People of Plenty," David Potter persuasively advances the thesis that the most distinguishing traits of national character have been fundamentally shaped by the abundance of the American living standard. He marshals evidence of the effect that plenty has had upon such decisive phases of life as the nursing and training of babies, opportunities for education and jobs, ages of marriage and childbearing. He shows how abundance has determined characteristic national attitudes between parents and children, husband and wife, superior and subordinate, between one class and another, and how it has moulded our mass culture and our consumer oriented society. American national character would indeed appear inconceivable without this unique experience of abundance.

The South has at times shared this national experience, and in very recent years has enjoyed more than a taste of it. But the history of the South includes a long and quite un-American experience with poverty. As recently as 1938, in fact, the South was characterized by the President as "The Nation's Economic Problem No. 1." And the problem was poverty, not plenty. It was a poverty emphasized by wide regional discrepancies in living standard, per capita wealth, per capita income, and the good things that money buys, such as education, health, protection, and the many luxuries that go to make up the celebrated American Standard of Living. This striking differential was no temporary misfortune of the great depression but a continuous and conspicuous feature of Southern experience since the early years of the Civil War. During the last half of the nineteenth and the first half of the twentieth centuries, when technology was multiplying American abundance with unprecedented rapidity, the South lagged far behind. In 1880 the per capita wealth of the South, based on estimated true valuation of property, was $376 as compared with $1,186 per capita in the states outside the South. In the same year the per capita wealth of the South was 27 per cent of that of the Northeastern states. That was just about the same ratio contemporaneously existing between the per capita wealth of Russia and that of Germany.

Generations of scarcity and want constitute one of the distinctive historical experiences of the Southern people, an experience too deeply embedded in their memory to be wiped out by a business boom and too deep not to admit of some uneasiness at being characterized historically as a "People of Plenty." That they should have been for so long a time a "People of Poverty" in a land of plenty is one mark of

enduring cultural distinctiveness. In a nation known around the world for the hedonistic ethic of the American Standard of Living, the Southern heritage of scarcity is distinctive.

A closely related corollary of the uniquely American experience of abundance is the equally unique American experience of success. Some years ago Arthur M. Schlesinger made an interesting attempt to define the national character which he brought to a close with the conclusion that the American character "is bottomed upon the profound conviction that nothing in the world is beyond its powers to accomplish." In this he gave expression to one of the great American legends, the legend of success and invincibility. It is a legend with a firm foundation in fact, for much can be adduced from the American record to support it and explain why it has flourished. If the history of the United States is lacking in some of the elements of variety and contrast demanded of any good story, it is in part because of the very monotonous repetitions of successes. Almost every major collective effort, even those thwarted temporarily, succeeded in the end. American history *is* a success story. Why should such a nation not have a "profound conviction that nothing in the world is beyond its power to accomplish"? Even the hazards of war—including the prospect of war against an unknown enemy with untried weapons—proves no exception to the rule. For these people have never known the chastening experience of being on the losing side of a war. They have solved every major problem they have confronted—or had it solved for them by a smiling fortune. Success and victory are national habits of mind.

This is but one among several American legends in which the South can participate only vicariously or in part. Again the Southern heritage is distinctive. For Southern history, unlike American, includes large components of frustration, failure, and defeat. It includes not only an overwhelming military defeat but long decades of defeat in the provinces of economic, social, and political life. Such a heritage affords the Southern people no basis for the delusion that there is nothing whatever that is beyond their power to accomplish. They have had it forcibly and repeatedly borne in upon them that this is not the case. Since their experience in this respect is more common among the general run of mankind that that of their fellow Americans, it would seem to be a part of their heritage worth cherishing.

American opulence and American success have combined to foster and encourage another legend of early origin, the legend of American innocence. According to this legend Americans achieved a sort of regeneration of sinful man by coming out of the wicked Old World and removing to an untarnished new one. By doing so they shook off the wretched evils of feudalism and broke free from tyranny, monarchism, aristocracy, and privilege—all those institutions which, in the hopeful philosophy of the Enlightenment, accounted for all, or nearly all, the evil in the world. The absence of these Old World ills in America, as well as the freedom from much of the injustice and oppression associated with them, encouraged a singular moral complacency in the American mind. The self-image implanted in Americans was one of innocence as compared with less fortunate people of the Old World. They were a chosen people and their land a Utopia on the make. De Tocqueville's patience was tried by this complacency of the American. "If I applaud the freedom which its inhabitants enjoy, he answers, 'Freedom is a fine thing, but few nations are worthy to enjoy it.' If I remark on the purity of morals which distinguishes the United States," complained Tocqueville, " 'I can imagine,' says he, 'that a stranger, who has been struck by corruption of all other nations, is astonished at the difference.' "

How much room was there in the tortured conscience of the South for this national self-image of innocence and moral complacency? Southerners have repeated the American rhetoric of self admiration and sung the perfection of American institutions ever since the Declaration of Independence. But for half that time they lived intimately with a great social evil and the other half with its aftermath. It was an evil that was even condemned and abandoned by the Old World, to which America's moral superiority was an article of faith. Much of the South's intellectual energy went into a desperate effort to convince the world that its peculiar evil was actually a "positive good," but it failed even to convince itself. It writhed in the torments of its own conscience until it plunged into catastrophe to escape. The South's preoccupation was with guilt, not with innocence, with the reality of evil, not with the dream of perfection. Its experience in this respect was on the whole a thoroughly un-American one.

An age-long experience with human bondage and its evils and later with emancipation and its shortcomings did not dispose the South very favorably toward such popular American ideas as the doctrine of human perfectibility, the belief that every evil has a cure, and the notion that every human problem has a solution. For these reasons the utopian schemes and the gospel of progress that flourished above the Mason and Dixon Line never found very wide acceptance below the Potomac during the nineteenth century. In that most optimistic of centuries in the most optimistic part of the world, the South remained basically pessimistic in its social outlook and its moral philosophy. The experience of evil and the experience of tragedy are parts of the Southern heritage that are as difficult to reconcile with the American legend of innocence and social felicity as the experience of poverty and defeat with the legends of abundance and success.

One of the simplest but most consequential generalizations ever made about national character was Tocqueville's, that America was "born free." In many ways that is the basic distinction between the history of the United States and the history of other great nations. We skipped the feudal stage, just as Russia skipped the liberal stage. Louis Hartz has pointed up the infinitely complex consequences for the history of American political thought. To be a conservative and a traditionalist in America was a contradiction in terms, for the American Burke was forever conserving John Locke's liberalism, his only real native tradition. Even the South in its great period of reaction against Jefferson was never able fully to shake off the grip of Locke and its early self-image of liberalism. That is why its most original period of theoretical inspiration, the "Reactionary Enlightenment," came such a complete cropper and left almost no influence upon American thought.

There is still a contribution to be derived from the South's un-American adventure in feudal fantasy. The South was born Lockeian, but, as Hartz admits, it was long "an alien child in a liberal family, tortured and confused, driven to a fantasy life." There *are* Americans, after all, who were not "born free." They are also Southerners. They have yet to achieve articulate expression of their uniquely un-American experience. This is not surprising, since white Southerners have only recently found expression of the tragic potentials of their past in literature. The Negro has yet to do that. His first step will be an acknowledgment that he is also a Southerner as well as an American.

One final example of a definition of national character to which the South proves an exception is an interesting one by Thornton Wilder. "Americans," says Mr. Wilder, "are abstract. They are disconnected. They have a relation, but it is to everywhere, to everybody, and to always." This quality of abstraction he finds expressed in numerous ways, in the physical mobility of Americans, in their indifference or, as he might suggest, their superi-

ority to place, to locality, to environment. "For us," he writes, "it is not *where* genius lived that is important. If Mount Vernon and Monticello were not so beautiful in themselves and relatively accessible, would so many of us visit them?" he asks. It is not the concrete but the abstract that captures the imagination of the American and gives him identity, not the here-and-now but the future. "'I am I,' he says, 'because my plans characterize me.' Abstract! Abstract!" Mr. Wilder's stress upon abstraction as an American characteristic recalls what Robert Penn Warren in a different connection once described as "the fear of abstraction" in the South, "the instinctive fear, on the part of black or white, that the massiveness of experience, the concreteness of life, will be violated; the fear of abstraction."

According to Mr. Wilder, "Americans can find in environment no confirmation of their identity, try as they may." And again, "Americans are disconnected. They are exposed to all place and all time. No place nor group nor movement can say to them: we are waiting for you; it is right for you to be here." The insignificance of place, locality, community for Thornton Wilder contrasts strikingly with the experience of Eudora Welty of Mississippi. "Like a good many other [regional] writers," she says, "I am myself touched off by place. The place where I am and the place I know, and other places that familiarity with and love for my own make strange and lovely and enlightening to look into, are what set me to writing my stories." To her "place opens a door in the mind," and she speaks of "the blessing of being located—contained."

To do Mr. Wilder justice, he is aware that the Southern states constitute an exception to his national character of abstraction, "enclaves or residual areas of European feeling," he calls them. "They were cut off, or resolutely cut themselves off, from the advancing tide of the country's modes of consciousness.

Place, environment, relations, repetitions are the breath of their being."

The most reassuring prospect for the survival of the South's distinctive heritage is the magnificent body of literature produced by its writers in the last three decades—the very years when the outward traits of regional distinctiveness were crumbling. The Southern literary renaissance has placed its writers in the vanguard of national letters and assured that their works will be read as long as American literature is remembered. The distinguishing feature of the Southern school, according to Allen Tate, is "the peculiar historical consciousness of the Southern writer." He defines the literary renaissance as "a literature conscious of the past in the present." The themes that have inspired the major writers have not been the flattering myths nor the romantic dreams of the South's past. Disdaining the polemics of defense and justification, they have turned instead to the somber realities of hardship and defeat and evil and "the problems of the human heart in conflict with itself." In so doing they have brought to realization for the first time the powerful literary potentials of the South's tragic experience and heritage. Such comfort as they offer lies, in the words of William Faulkner, in reminding us of "the courage and honor and hope and pride and compassion and pity and sacrifice" with which man has endured.

After Faulkner and Wolfe and Warren and Welty no literate Southerner could remain unaware of his heritage or doubt its enduring value. After this outpouring it would seem more difficult than ever to deny a Southern identity, to be "merely American." To deny it would be to deny our history. And it would also be to deny to America participation in a heritage and a dimension of historical experience that America very much needs, a heritage that is far more closely in line with the common lot of mankind than the national legends of opulence and success and innocence. The South once thought of itself as a "peculiar people," set apart by its eccentricities, but in many ways modern America better deserves that description.

The South was American a long time before it was Southern in any self-conscious or distinctive way. It remains more American by far than anything else and has all along. After all, it fell to the lot of one Southerner to define America. The definition that he wrote voiced aspirations that were deeply rooted in his native region before the nation was born. The modern Southerner should be secure enough in his national identity to escape the compulsion of less secure minorities to embrace uncritically all the myths of nationalism. He should be secure enough also not to deny a regional heritage because it is at variance with national myth. It is a heritage that should prove of enduring worth to him as well as to his country.

JAMES JACKSON KILPATRICK (b. 1920) is editor of the Richmond (Virginia) *News Leader*. In editorials, essays, and articles this vocal southerner espouses states' rights and a strict interpretation of the United States Constitution, deploring the influence of those whom he considers to be weakening the foundations of the Republic. He takes a similar stand in two books, *The Sovereign States: Notes of a Citizen of Virginia* (1957) and *The Southern Case for School Segregation* (1962). In this essay Kilpatrick argues that the South is the nation's last bastion of the conservative cause in the United States—a cause that he favors without apology.*

James Jackson Kilpatrick

A Conservative Political Philosophy

"By and Large," wrote Russell Kirk in *The Conservative Mind*, "radical thinkers have won the day. For a century and a half, conservatives have yielded ground in a manner which, except for occasionally successful rear-guard actions, must be described as a rout."

The Southern States, at mid-century, find themselves very nearly alone in fighting this rear-guard action against the legions of Change, the armies of a supposed Enlightenment. They represent, collectively, the last and best hope of conservatism in the American Republic. If the conservative cause is to survive at all in the United States, as a political philosophy, as an approach to the perplexing problems of our restless and edgy civil-ization, it will be largely because a body of tradition exists within the South and will not lie down.

It is useful to consider this hypothesis, whether it is so; and if it is so, why it is so. What is it about the South that has made the South, historically and presently, a bastion of conservatism? It is profitable to think upon the value of a conservative force, if it has value; to search out the meaning of "conservatism," its Southern roots and branches; and to examine the function of the Southern conservative in a society both antagonistic to the South and hostile to the conservative spirit.

One may begin, and there is splendidly pessimistic tradition for doing so, by ob-

---

*James Jackson Kilpatrick, "Conservatism and the South," in Louis J. Rubin, Jr., and James Jackson Kilpatrick (eds.), *The Lasting South* (Chicago: Henry Regnery Company, 1957), pp. 188–205.

serving that the Southern conservative's lot, these days, is not a happy one. This is not because of the "race issue" alone: It is no more proper to assert that every Southern States' righter of the mid-twentieth century is "pro-segregation" than it was proper, a hundred years ago, to charge that every States' righter of that day was "pro-slavery" or even "pro-secession." Alexander Stephens, in the Georgia of 1860, struggled to keep Georgia in the Union but defended to his death her right to secede from it; similarly, a number of Southern conservatives today entertain, privately or publicly, strong doubts of the wisdom of a rigid racial segregation, but they will assert vigorously the right of a State to exercise its reserved police powers in this regard.

There is more to the defensive posture of the Southern conservative than this. Conservatism generally is unpopular, and the antipathy rubs off on the South. Two factors, one instinctive, the other semantic, are in part responsible for the conservative's repeated setbacks.

Instinctively, it seems to me, the American is a dissatisfied, critical person. Curiosity, rebellion, experimentation—these are built into his gene string; and from many standpoints, it is well that this is so. A great republic has arisen from the conviction of energetic men that the grass must be greener somewhere else. In the natural order of things, the apostles crying "go!" are always more numerous, or at least more articulate, than the prophets crying "stay!" As a result, the conservative suggestion to look is derided by men who would leap; and because we are by nature a passionate people, much given to epithet and insult, the custom is to fall upon conservative spokesmen as fascists, bigots and reactionaries. The words don't mean anything in particular, but they keep the adrenals flowing.

And because other words have lost their meaning, the conservative finds a major se-

mantic obstacle squarely in his path. His opponent is popularly known—God save the mark!—as the *liberal.* It is a graceful word, of fine and shining connotations; it evokes the Latin *liberalis,* it sings of men once liberated from tyrant's grasp, it suggests all things characteristic of liberty and generosity and freedom. Yet by every precept of political philosophy, it is the conservative of our day who expounds and defends the truly liberal principle; it is the conservative who would free man from the needless restrictions and regimentation of the state. In some bewilderment and frustration, the conservative acknowledges that his opponents have kidnaped his word; in self-defense, he is compelled to wage war against "liberals" and "liberalism," and his efforts to label the opposition as "Socialists" or "statists" seem not to have taken hold. As a result, the conservative is tagged as selfish, the liberal as bountiful. And who shoots at Santa Claus? The enemy camp knows a good thing when it sees it, and the "liberal" label is too good to let go.

Thus the misconception of the American conservative takes shape: He is seen as a stingy fellow, long-faced, cautious, timid. He wears rubbers when the sun is shining, remembering sudden rains; he is prudently clad in both suspenders and belt, against the possibility of embarrassment should one or the other fail. He moves, when he moves at all, with grudging slowness. He is a Jeremiah forever wailing in the habitations of the wilderness, a wet-blanket, a Milquetoast, a bore. Or in another version, beloved of Mr. Block of the Washington *Post,* he is a fat and bloated fellow, unjustly rich (you know he is unjustly rich because he is smoking a ceegar); his rapacious eye seeks out the "giveaway." You find him trodding upon the lissome maid of Hawaiian Statehood; you see his uncouth and selfish features leering happily at the sight of little children jammed in an overcrowded schoolhouse. In either version, as the funereal prophet of doom or the bumptious apostle of profit, this misconceived conservative is a most unattractive fellow.

Is this wretched being in truth a "conservative"? Are timidity and selfishness the tenets of "conservatism"? Of course not. Lincoln defined the philosophy briefly as "adherence to the old and tried, against the new and untried," but that is too brief. It is true, of course, as Kirk has noted, that the conservative seeks in general "to stand by tradition and old establishments," and "to preserve the ancient moral traditions of humanity." Doubtless the conservative, more than others, exhibits what Gibbon called "the propensity of mankind to exalt the past and deprecate the present." But I have never comprehended that conservatism is ancestor worship and nothing more; nor have I believed that the "old and tried" is necessarily, in every instance, superior to the "new and untried." Sometimes it is no better to honor age in government than in eggs.

By conservatism, I mean a philosophy predicated upon the conviction that certain eternal verities exist; that these truths endure, or should endure, and that respect is due them. Conservatism assumes a divine power, unknown and unknowable, which has created man and equipped him with reason and intellect and will. The conservative recognizes that not all men have the same capacity for reason and intellect, and he knows that if free will is to have fullest meaning, it must embrace both the rewards of success and the penalties of failure. Thus the conservative repudiates the notion that all men are equal, for he sees that demonstrably this is not so; he would not have it otherwise. Conservatism is patient; it perceives that change and progress are not necessarily the same things. Conservatism is prudent; it finds it better, in general, to bear the ills we have than fly to others that we know not of. Conservatism is strong; it holds that a house can be no better than its foundations, and it proposes to build on rock, not sand.

Ceaselessly, the conservative urges that individual man is entitled to the greatest possible liberty consistent with order and responsibility. Here he would not be misunderstood. He does not equate liberty with license. He believes, with Webster, that "liberty exists in proportion to wholesome restraint," and that a profligate excess of freedom will bring the retribution any other profligacy exacts.

Conservatism asks also not to be misunderstood on a closely related point: The conservative is not, as is often said, simply "agin the guv'mint," or opposed to all government. Of course he is not. He recalls what Henry said in the Virginia Convention of 1788, that in creating a government it is best to proceed on the assumption that men will be bad, for it is likely they will be so; thus he accepts the necessity for government, to preserve law, order and property from forces antagonistic to society. This is the first reason for government, as Calhoun observed, to restrain men, just as it is the first reason for constitutions, to restrain governments. Far from opposing law, conservatism insists upon preserving law. It is only through the processes of law, as the conservative above all men must recognize, that the stability of his institutions may be preserved from "the lust for innovation," in Randolph's phrase, that has been the death of all republics.

To say that conservatism respects a divine intent, that it fosters responsible liberty, that it defends sound tradition and upholds order and classes against the leveling goals of the welfare state, is to suggest, per contra, the things that conservatism opposes: Secularism, an impersonal industrialism, most of all (and it is with this evil that the Southern conservative is most concerned) the statism which tends steadily to overwhelm this republic and to destroy the fabric of federal union.

By secularism I mean something more than merely a decline in religious emphasis or simple piety, though this is part of it: A people who in 1776 appealed to the "Supreme Judge of the World" for the rectitude of their intentions, and placed their firm reliance in a Divine Providence, seem to have mislaid this faith in a Power larger than themselves. Our coins still assert that it is in God we trust, but I wonder if it is so. More broadly, the conservative aligns himself against the materialism and the false values of a society which pays the plumber half-again what it pays the school teacher, considering it more important to have toilets that flush smoothly than children who think clearly. When a football coach draws twice the salary of a professor of philosophy, and alumni buy tackles but seldom buy microscopes, something is wrong. More and more we seem to live in a spiritual Levittown. If our intellects soared as high as our TV antennae—but never mind: The conservative finds that enduring moral values, old precepts of taste and manners and familial right conduct, are beset at every hand; and he struggles for their preservation. . . .

What the conservative fears, and rightly so, is the blind veneration of bigness which industrialism exacts of its worshippers. More than others, perhaps, the conservative senses the magnitude of the sacrifices laid before smokestacks. He would not, of course, have the economy return to hand-looms and water-ground meal, nor is he suggesting that much in modern industry is not fine and admirable. What he objects to is the wholesale decline in old ideals—old concepts of craftsmanship, of the inherent value of work, of pride in individual accomplishment. Is time-and-a-half, he asks, the ultimate reward of life here on earth? And is not a terrible mockery afoot when 10,000 union members, striving to preserve the closed shop in Indiana, strike a *liberty bell* as the symbol of their tyrannical

aim? Industry, in the old meaning of the word, in the root meaning that gives us *industrious,* is undoubtedly good. It is when industry passes into industrialism, into a social organization dominated by the cult of production, that men are reduced to punchcards and the fruit of their genius to statistical units of output. In the drawings of Artzybasheff, one finds the great body-presses of Dearborn cast ominously in images of old Aztec gods, ugly, imperious and powerful; and the conservative reflects that the conveyor belt which brings material riches carries away something of the spirit, too.

To a remarkable extent, it seems to me, the South traditionally has reflected the conservative position in these matters. For all the astonishing growth of Southern industry in recent years, the region remains basically agrarian in its politics, its economy, its outlook. Ours is still pretty much a land of small farms; and though the number of small farmers is declining, their influence remains strong in our councils of state. This attitude of cautious reserve toward industrialism is allied with the Southerner's love of place, and his sense of community; it has its roots in a tradition of man's dependence on the soil and his independence by reason of this. The factory may or may not be permanent; the land *is.* Pines, not chimneys, loom large in the horizon of his recollection. "Conservatism," says Kirk, "always has had its most loyal adherents in the country." And country is the one thing we have most of.

Similarly, the South to this day preserves its deep devotion to things of the spirit, as distinguished from those of the flesh. To be sure, we have sinned against our old gods: The South has its Levittowns, its underpaid teachers, its share of greedy men; our institutions of higher education have suffered the corrosive effects of over-emphasized football. . . . And yet . . . and yet . . . secularism and materialism have not made the inroads in the

South that one witnesses elsewhere, and for good reason. It is said, sometimes scoffingly, that we live in the "Bible Belt," in a land of fundamentalist preachers whose people pray to an anthropomorphic God; but if this sometimes results in a Scopes trial or in the rituals of hill country Faith healers, it more often results in a simple and homely faith, in a certainty of salvation and a fear of divine wrath. Southerners are a prayerful people. It is not without significance that in rewriting the very preamble of the Federal Constitution, to adapt it to the Confederate States, the framers of 1860 carefully declared their purpose to establish justice, insure domestic tranquility, secure the blessings of liberty— and then, with solid tradition behind them, inserted a respectful phrase: "Invoking the favor and guidance of Almighty God," they ordained and established a Constitution for the Confederate States of America.

The Southern tradition acknowledges the failure of this invocation. . . . [T]he South has known defeat—as no other region has known it. Tragically, palpably, the South saw her prayers spurned, her land ravished, a terrible penance put upon her. In the process, our people came to know the lean and bony face of poverty; we know it still. Lacking outside diversions, the Southerner has been compelled to search within himself; and there he has found a realization, not so widely discovered elsewhere, that money in fact isn't everything. This is not only because there live in the relatively moneyless South a great many people who don't have it and can't earn it, but because a different tradition of values governs our society. There remains in the South an innate code of honor, an inheritance of manners, a certain sense of fitness, an easy patience often misunderstood as indolence.

These are subtle things, not easily defined; but the Southerner senses them daily—in the Virginian's incessant "sir," the Mississippian's deference to women, the courtesies of Kentucky. He knows that efficiency is not necessarily the finest attribute of men or society; that it is not imperative to accomplish all things today, or tomorrow, or even day after tomorrow. Toward the end of the War of 1861–65, South Carolina undertook to build a new state house at Columbia; Sherman's artillerymen amused themselves by firing on the structure, and metal stars, set in the granite, still mark where the balls landed. In the embarrassment of the time, unable to complete the Capitol, South Carolina erected only a temporary dome on top. The dome has been temporary, now, for nearly a hundred years. But life in Columbia is exceedingly pleasant, and South Carolinians do not complain.

The conservatism of the American South, I have submitted, thus exhibits to an unusual degree the characteristics by which the conservative philosophy generally is identified: An indwelling devotion to tradition and good manners, a resistance to industrialism, a coolness to the secularist sirens who sing of material pleasures. But there is, of course, one thing more than this, the political tradition of the South with which this essay is primarily concerned. This is the South's abiding, unyielding opposition to centralism, and to the dead hand of the impassive state. In terms of constitutional exposition, we know it as the doctrine of States' Rights. And at mid-century, that doctrine is flourishing with fresh vitality and renewed conviction.

For the past several years, many of us in the South have been doing our frustrated best to educate the great world outside in a few fundamental truths about the Constitution and what is happening to that beloved compact. Try as we may, the task is rough going. When the literate Southern conservative—and there are some literate Southern conservatives— seeks access to the major media of national communication, he finds the borders closed to him as though he carried typhoid. . . .

Now   and   then   Southern   spokesmen

produce a little noise; now and then a Southern missionary is permitted to cross over Jordan, in order to acquaint college sophomores of New England and the Upper Midwest with "the other side." Such junkets are at once exhilarating and depressing: After months of sitting with fiddle at rest, overwhelmed by the din of liberal timpani and impatiently asking "now?", "now?", the Southern States' Righter finds it good to play a few solo measures. But lecturing on the Tenth Amendment before these bright-eyed students is like plowing fresh clay. The Fifth Amendment—that, yes, the Fifth they have heard of. But the Tenth? Theirs is a generation that knows not Joseph. The Tenth Amendment, the Doctrine of '98, the demonstrable basis of State sovereignty—these things are mysteries to be ranked with quantum physics and the French subjunctive.

Yet there is nothing obscure about the States' Righter's concept of the Constitution. The gospel does not demand of its disciples that they be metaphysicians or constitutional lawyers either; it asks only that they read and comprehend the English language. What the States' Righter says is that if the Constitution be read from beginning to end, just as it came from Philadelphia late in the summer of 1787, from "We the people" in the preamble to the final ratifying clause of Article VII, it will be perfectly apparent that what the States created was a federal union of separate sovereign States, each individual, each State (as the Tenth Amendment makes clear) *respectively* possessed of all powers not delegated to the general government by the Constitution nor denied by the Constitution to the States. That is not so difficult a doctrine. . . .

If nine States ratified, the Constitution would be binding as to them. But if Virginia, New York, North Carolina and Rhode Island had failed to ratify—they were Numbers 10, 11, 12, and 13—the United States of America would have come into being anyway; and Virginia, New York, North Carolina and Rhode Island might be to this day as politically separate as any Luxembourg or Belgium. Under the Articles of Confederation, the States had asserted nothing so explicitly as their separate, individual sovereignty. This sovereignty they retained under the Constitution of 1787. Whenever three fourths of the States wish to do so (whether or not the three fourths contain a majority or a minority of the whole population), they may wipe out Congress, provide for a dual executive, dissolve the Supreme Court, or make any other change they please. This power to make and unmake is what is meant by sovereignty; and it resides not in the people as people en masse, but in the people-as-States.

Paraphrasing Holy Writ, it may be said of the sovereign States: Before the Union was, we *are*. Madison put it this way in *The Federalist:* "Each State," he said, "in ratifying the Constitution, is considered as a sovereign body, independent of all others, and only to be bound by its voluntary act." The volition to bind certainly would appear to embrace the volition to unbind. A sovereign people, capable of exercising the power to ratify, must also possess the power to rescind. This was the sound reasoning advanced by the Southern States in 1860; it is sound reasoning today, and until the Constitution be rewritten to abolish the States, it will remain a sound position. The bloody war of 1861–65 did not prove the North right as a matter of law, only superior as a matter of arms. It also follows from this line of reasoning that the States which are parties to the mutual compact should be, in the last resort, the final judges of its violation. When the final arbitrament of contested powers is effectively conceded to the Supreme Court, an agency of the general government, and as such an agency created by the States themselves, the agent becomes superior to the master. In that moment of concession, the whole structure and meaning of our government are distorted; the people within their States no longer are sovereign—

the court has effectively assumed sovereign power, and we exchange government by the people for government by judicial oligarchy.

The Southern States' Righter does not plead his case on the law alone, but on the merits also. He cherishes the conviction—it is an age-old conviction in the South—that strong State governments are infinitely more to be desired than a strong central government. He knows the people can restrain government when government is close at hand. At the State level, the reins of power run straight from hand to bit: Citizens of Virginia alone choose a Governor of Virginia and an Assembly that acts for Virginia alone. Jefferson's Capitol at Richmond offers both a political and spiritual home, to be possessed with a fierce sense of exclusive possession.

In sharp contrast to this friendly closeness of State government, the Southern conservative soberly contemplates a central government which grows increasingly more remote. He cannot untangle the harness that once was expected to control the creature. Responsibility here is diffuse; everybody is accountable and nobody is accountable. Who is the rider, who the ridden? He journeys to Washington and finds the committees of Congress full of strangers; the vastness of marble hearing rooms reduces the intimacy of his own chambers at the State Capitol to a shabby insignificance. He visits Washington not casually, as master, but suppliantly, as servant; and he uneasily comprehends that his most personal domestic affairs have become subject to the authority of men politically beyond his reach. His Federal government seems no longer to derive just power from the consent of the governed; he does not recall delegating such vast powers. Power, he recognizes, has simply been assumed. And the conservative passionately conceives this to be wrong.

This dedication to the essential rightness of State responsibility, this concept of the State

as the basic political entity of the American structure, is as old as the South itself. It was a favorite thesis of Jefferson, who saw the assertion of State powers as a great bulwark against the one calamity he feared even more than disunion—the greatest calamity of all, "submission to a government of unlimited powers." He believed steadfastly that "the States can best govern our home concerns."

In their original resolutions of ratification, the Southern States made this view explicit. . . .

State resolutions promptly resulted in the Tenth Amendment. This amendment consists of a single sentence, only twenty-eight words long; it is in no way obscure. *The powers* (not rights, as in the Ninth Amendment, but powers) *not delegated to the United States* (the verb is delegated, not "surrendered," or "granted," or "vested in," but merely delegated) *by the Constitution* (not by inference, or by any notions of inherent powers, but by the Constitution alone), *nor prohibited by it to the States* (prohibited by the Constitution, that is, by its specific limitations, and not by mandate of any court or Congress or executive, but only by the Constitution itself), *are reserved to the States respectively* (not to the States jointly, but to the States individually and respectively), *or to the people* (because there may be some powers the people will not wish to entrust even to their States).

This is the ark of the covenant. And whether the Tenth Amendment is read in the context of 1790, or as a living, vital part of the Constitution today, its meaning is perfectly clear: The sole powers of the Federal government are powers delegated to it by the States through the Constitution; and all powers not delegated, or prohibited by the Constitution to the States, are reserved to the States separately to be exercised by them—*for good or ill*—according to the wishes of the people within their States.

I emphasise "for good or ill," because this right of individual States to do what other States may regard as wrong is essential to any understanding of the Federal Union. The diversity of beliefs across this broad land, the infinite variety of local conditions and problems and traditions which contribute to diverse political viewpoints, form an enduring characteristic of the United States of America. All the miracles of communication and transportation cannot wipe out this diversity, nor substitute a regimented oneness in its place. Is legalized gambling wrong? It is Nevada's right to sanction it if she pleases. Was it wrong to permit the distillation and sale of whisky? Many persons thought so, but it did not become constitutionally a wrong until the long dark night of prohibition descended in 1920. Is it "good" for 18-year-olds to vote? Georgia thinks so, and that is Georgia's right and power. In this Republic, what the States choose to do in their reserved fields is their own business, *for good or ill,* until the Constitution itself be amended by the States themselves to establish a rule applicable to all alike.

The abiding prayer of many Southern conservatives is that this individuality and responsibility be preserved; their continuing apprehension is that local government will be reduced to impotence by gradual consolidation, and the States in essence will be destroyed by judicial erosion. This is seen as a perversion of law, but more than this: It is seen as a surrender to a remote statism, a submission to some massive Orwellian control too powerful ever to be restrained. There is a tyranny of the majority. Nothing was recognized more clearly than this when the Union was formed, and a dozen provisions were inserted in the Constitution to forestall it. Now these provisions are being circumvented or ignored; and this is being done, as Plato long ago imagined it would be done, in the name of liberty: "Tyranny springs from democracy,"

he said, when liberty magnified and intensified overmasters necessary restraints against license. "The excess of liberty, whether in States or indivuduals, seems only to pass into excess of slavery." Understanding this, conservatism pleads for a system of government kept close to the people governed, subject to their wishes, responsive to what they perceive to be their own needs. This is the sort of government envisioned by the wise men, genius-struck, who fashioned our Constitution. We will abandon it at our peril.

This body of political tradition, cherished in the South of Jefferson, Calhoun, Upshur, Stephens, Byrd, and Byrnes, underlies the resistance of Southern States to the Supreme Court's decree in the school segregation cases. . . . What happened on May 17, 1954, was that the Supreme Court undertook to accomplish by judicial fiat what the Tenth Amendment declares can be accomplished by the Constitution alone: The court undertook to prohibit the States from exercising a power they had reserved to themselves respectively. This is not "interpretation" of the Constitution; to all practical intents and purposes, it is substantive amendment of the Constitution, and the power to amend lies not with the court, but solely with three fourths of the States. . . .

It had been my intention to offer a justification, on the merits, of school segregation in the South. The two years between conception and publication have served to convince me, a dozen times over, that such justification exists, but these two years have also persuaded me that in the present climate of opinion, it would be useless to propound it. Such is the emotional frenzy created by our antagonists that considerations of reason, observation, and experience would be speedily shouted down. . . .

The constitutional question is something else entirely, and here the Southern conservative hopes keenly to win support beyond his homeland. Wholly aside from the merits of school segregation as such, divorced from "moral" or "Christian" considerations, there stands a formidable problem in constitutional law. What are the limits, if any, upon the power of the Supreme Court to "interpret" the Constitution? Where in a government of checks and balances can one find an effective check upon the court? If the individual justices' "sense of judicial self-restraint" is in fact the only rein upon the court, has not a government of law been abandoned to a government of men?

These are questions of far-reaching importance, transcending the immediate issue of school segregation in the Southern States. Thoughtful attorneys eleswhere, no friends of segregation, are troubled by the trend; and in a calmer day, when it may be possible to criticize the court without being labeled "anti-Negro," more of them will speak frankly of the violence done to the stability of law on May 17, 1954. Viewed strictly from a constitutional standpoint, the South's position is basically sound and right. Regardless of what happens in Southern schools, that position ultimately will be vindicated.

It will be vindicated or the whole nature of this Republic will be drastically changed—and I believe, changed for the worse. The United States will cease to be a union of individual States, and will become instead a consolidated nation. Virtually all government will center in Washington. The responsibilities of State and local administrations will dwindle to the merest sweeping of streets, the clipping of public parks. Immense, unapproachable, unreachable, the monolithic structure of Federal government will dominate men's lives and control their destinies. Already we are far advanced toward subjection to the omniscient state.

If this leveling sweep of the bulldozer society can be checked at all, it will be checked by a vigorous conservative force—by counter influences pleading the cause of individual responsibilities within an incentive society, by political leadership advancing the constitutional prerogatives of the States. Such an incipient force exists now within the South. The conservative instinct survives there; it survives not strongly, but at least stubbornly, and it offers a brake upon a society plunging rapidly into a statism only dimly forseen.

"The empire of Rome," Gibbon tells us, "was firmly established by the singular and perfect coalition of its members." So, too, was our own Republic. And "the decline of Rome," Gibbon adds, "was the natural and inevitable effect of immoderate greatness." Not of greatness: Of *immoderate* greatness, of excesses of power and wealth and envy and ambition, of a lust for authority that must consume freedom in its flames. We can follow Rome. If the forces of conservatism are obliterated, that melancholy end will soon be inescapable; we will have traded the rights of man for the dispensations of the state, and found the pursuit of happiness an illusory blind alley that leads to nothing at all. If the lasting South can prevent this, or help to prevent it, the influence of Southern conservatism one day will be counted not bigotry but blessing. There, men may say, was the anchor by which we rode out the storm.

Suggested Readings

The South has attracted the attention of innumerable writers, and every indicator points to a continual flow of publication of regional studies. The following bibliography is a highly selected list of recently published volumes readily available for additional reading on the South. Some of the volumes listed here were not written as conscious attempts to advance a regional thesis, or theme, but all of them may be read with profit by one who desires to understand the essence of Southernism.

Arthur S. Link and Rembert W. Patrick (eds.), *Writing Southern History: Essays in Historiography in Honor of Fletcher M. Green* (Baton Rouge, 1965), containing seventeen interpretive essays by well-known scholars, is a detailed and systematic study of Southern historical literature, ranging from the colonial period to the twentieth century. Useful surveys of the entire scope of Southern history are provided by Francis B. Simkins, *A History of the South* (3d ed.; New York, 1963) and William B. Hesseltine and David L. Smiley, *The South in American History* (2d ed.; Englewood Cliffs, N.J., 1960). The Old South and Confederacy are treated by Clement Eaton in *A History of the Old South* (2d ed.; New York, 1966), *The Growth of Southern Civilization, 1790–1860* (New York, 1961), and *A History of the Southern Confederacy* (New York, 1954); and the New South has been surveyed by John S. Ezell, *The South Since 1865* (New York, 1963) and Thomas D. Clark and Albert D. Kirwan, *The South Since Appomattox* (New York, 1967).

Detailed and valuable is the cooperative History of the South series, under the editorship of Wendell Holmes Stephenson and E. Merton Coulter. This series is sponsored jointly by the University of Texas and Louisiana State University and published by the press of the latter. All titles of this ten-volume series are recommended: Wesley Frank Craven, *The Southern Colonies in the Seventeenth Century, 1607–1689* (1949); Clarence Ver Steeg, *The Southern Colonies in the Eighteenth Century, 1689–1763* (to be published); John Richard Alden, *The South in the Revolution, 1763–1789* (1957); Thomas P. Abernethy, *The South in the New Nation, 1789–1819* (1961); Charles S. Sydnor, *The Development of Southern Sectionalism, 1819–1848* (1948); Avery O. Craven, *The Growth of Southern Nationalism, 1848–1861* (1953); E. Merton Coulter, *The Confederate States of America, 1861–1865* (1950) and *The South During Reconstruction, 1865–1877* (1947); C. Vann Woodward, *Origins of the New South, 1877–1913* (1951); and George B. Tindall, *The Emergence of the New South, 1913–1945* (1967).

The institution of slavery greatly affected Southern life, and it has been the theme for a number of outstanding studies. Ulrich B. Phillips, *American Negro Slavery* (New York, 1918) and *Life and Labor in The Old South* (Boston, 1929) are old but valuable studies of slavery, although Phillips was too sympathetic to the institution. For more recent and more critical approaches, see Kenneth M. Stampp, *The Peculiar Institution: Slavery in the Ante-Bellum South* (New York, 1956); Stanley M. Elkins, *Slavery: A Problem in American Institutional and Intellectual Life* (Chicago, 1949); and Eugene Genovese, *The Political Economy of Slavery* (New York, 1965). Specifically directed toward the Southern slave system are Charles S. Sydnor, *Slavery in Mississippi* (New York, 1933) and Joe Gray Taylor, *Negro Slavery in Louisiana* (Baton Rouge, 1963). A well-written study of the transformation of the Sea Island Negroes from slaves to free citizens under the guidance of Northern abolitionist teachers is *Rehearsal for Reconstruction: The Port Royal Experiment* (New York, 1964) by Willie Lee Rose. A path-breaking study is Richard C. Wade,

Slavery in the Cities: The South, 1820–1860 (New York, 1964). William W. Freehling, *Prelude to Civil War: The Nullification Controversy in South Carolina, 1816–1836* (New York and London, 1966) makes a strong case for slavery as the central issue in the dispute over nullification.

The following are valuable for studies of the post-Civil War Negro: Vernon L. Wharton, *The Negro in Mississippi, 1865–1890* (Chapel Hill, N.C., 1947); George B. Tindall, *South Carolina Negroes, 1877–1900* (Columbia, S.C., 1952); Charles E. Wynes, *Race Relations in Virginia, 1870–1902* (Charlottesville, Va., 1961); Frenise A. Logan, *The Negro in North Carolina, 1876–1894* (Chapel Hill, N.C., 1964), and Joel Williamson, *After Slavery: The Negro in South Carolina During Reconstruction* (Chapel Hill, N.C., 1965). An original study of the beginnings and development of racial segregation in the South is C. Vann Woodward, *The Strange Career of Jim Crow* (2d ed.; New York, 1966). Other meritorious studies related to the Negro include: Rayford W. Logan, *The Negro in American Life and Thought* (New York, 1954); August Meier, *Negro Thought in America, 1880–1915* (Ann Arbor, Mich., 1963); and I. A. Newby, *Jim Crow's Defense: Anti-Negro Thought in America, 1900–1930* (Baton Rouge, 1965). An excellent survey of the Negro in American and Southern life is John Hope Franklin, *From Slavery to Freedom, A History of American Negroes* (New York, 1947), and a brief but superb summary of recent scholarship in Negro history is August Meier and Elliott M. Rudwick, *From Plantation to Ghetto: An Interpretive History of American Negroes* (New York, 1966).

Early Southern society and its ramifications have been the subjects of a number of writers. Louis B. Wright, *The First Gentlemen of Virginia: Intellectual Qualities of the Early Colonial Ruling Class* (San Marino, Calif., 1940) stresses the importance of a cavalier tradition as a source of continuing vitality in Southern colonial society, but Thomas J. Wertenbaker, *The Old South: The Founding of American Civilization* (New York, 1942) deprecates the concept of a pre-eminent aristocracy. Carl Bridenbaugh, *Myths and Realities: Societies of the Colonial South* (Baton Rouge, 1952) contends that the South as an entity did not exist in colonial times and that the heterogeneous

people living south of Pennsylvania were not consciously southerners. In a slim volume called *The First South* (Baton Rouge, 1961), John R. Alden writes that the South first appeared between 1775 and 1789 in opposition to the first North. Charles Sydnor, *Gentlemen Freeholders: Political Practices in Washington's Virginia* (Chapel Hill, N.C., 1952) sees the wealthy and well-born dominating society and politics of colonial Virginia, but this view is sharply challenged by Robert E. and Katherine B. Brown in *Virginia, 1705–1786: Democracy or Aristocracy?* (East Lansing, Mich., 1964). Jack P. Greene, *The Quest for Power: The Lower Houses of Assembly in the Southern Royal Colonies, 1689–1776* (Chapel Hill, N.C., 1963) is mainly political in emphasis, but much knowledge of Southern society may be gained from it.

Historians have given much attention to the attitudes and thoughts of southerners as a way to understand the region and its inhabitants. Wilbur J. Cash, *The Mind of the South* (New York, 1941) is already a minor classic. Volumes especially designed to explain the mind of the ante-bellum southerner are: Clement Eaton, *The Mind of the Old South* (rev. ed.; Baton Rouge, 1967), and *Freedom of Thought in the Old South* (New York, 1964); Rollin G. Osterweis, *Romanticism and Nationalism in the Old South* (New Haven, 1949); and William R. Taylor, *Cavalier and Yankee: The Old South and American National Character* (New York, 1961), a brilliant study of the myths of Southern and American culture. The thesis of David Bertelson, *The Lazy South* (New York, 1967) is that the distinguishing attribute among southerners was their lack of social unity. Another recent volume, Earl E. Thorpe, *Eros and Freedom in Southern Life and Thought* (Durham, N.C., 1967), was written to prove that little repression existed in the Old South, and since freedom is maximized where repression is minimized, the central theme of Southern history has been freedom. Douglas Southall Freeman, *R. E. Lee: A Biography* (4 vols.; New York, 1934–1935) is a detailed study of the man who epitomized what the South thinks its central themes to be.

Three volumes of essays illuminating the nuances of the mind of the recent southerner are: C. Vann Woodward, *The Burden of Southern History* (Baton Rouge, 1960); Charles G. Sellers, Jr. (ed.), *The Southerner as American* (Chapel

Hill, N.C., 1960); and Frank E. Vandiver (ed.), *The Idea of the South* (Chicago, 1964). Also helpful are two works by Southern-born Robert Penn Warren: *Segregation: The Inner Conflict in the South* (New York, 1956) and *The Legacy of the Civil War* (New York, 1961); the latter, deceptive because of its brevity, is filled with much understanding of the post-Civil War and twentieth-century generation. In *The Southern Mystique* (New York, 1964), Howard Zinn uses both historical and contemporary evidence to demonstrate that the racial prejudice of the twentieth-century Southern mind is not instinctive and that it can be altered. Perhaps the best recent book on the contemporary Negro issue is Charles E. Silberman, *Crisis in Black and White* (New York, 1964).

For the importance and influence of agriculture and agrarian traditions upon the southerner, see Theodore Saloutos, *Farmer Movements in the South, 1865–1933* (Berkeley, Calif., 1960); Willard Range, *A Century of Georgia Agriculture, 1850–1950* (Athens, Ga., 1954); Carl C. Taylor, *The Farmer's Movement, 1620–1920* (New York, 1953); and Fred S. Shannon, *American Farmers' Movements* (Princeton, 1957). *I'll Take My Stand* (New York, 1930), written by twelve southerners who decried the passing of the old agrarian society, is a must for every reader desiring to probe the Southern mind of the twentieth century.

Paul H. Buck, *The Road to Reunion, 1865–1900* (Boston, 1937) and C. Vann Woodward, *Reunion and Reaction: The Compromise of 1877 and the End of Reconstruction* (Boston, 1951) arrive at divergent conclusions concerning sectional reconciliation, but both remain valuable for the study of the South's postwar politics and society. Albert D. Kirwan, *Revolt of the Rednecks: Mississippi Politics, 1876–1925* (Lexington, Ky., 1951) is a sound revisionist study of post-Reconstruction politics. A major study of modern Southern politics and institutions is V. O. Key, Jr., *Southern Politics in State and Nation* (New York, 1949). Complementing Key's volume is Alexander Heard, *A Two-Party South?* (Chapel Hill, N.C., 1952). Two brief but excellent interpretive works are T. Harry Williams, *Romance and Realism in Southern Politics* (Athens, Ga., 1961) and Dewey W. Grantham, Jr., *The Demo-*

cratic South (Athens, Ga., 1963). Oriented toward Southern political behavior are: Cortez A. M. Ewing, *Primary Elections in the South: A Study in Uniparty Politics* (Norman, Okla., 1953); Taylor Cole and John H. Hallowell (eds.), *The Southern Political Scene, 1938–1948* (Gainesville, Fla., 1948); Donald S. Strong, *Urban Republicanism in the South* (University, Ala., 1960); and Jasper B. Shannon, *Toward A New Politics in the South* (Knoxville, Tenn., 1949). *Negroes and the New Southern Politics* (New York, Chicago, and Burlingame, Calif., 1966) by Donald R. Matthews and James W. Prothro is a massive volume by two social scientists whose research explodes certain firmly rooted myths and assumptions concerning the recently enfranchized Southern Negro.

Volumes that point up recent changes in the South include: Thomas D. Clark, *The Emerging South* (New York, 1961); Robert B. Highsaw (ed.), *The Deep South Transformation* (University, Ala., 1964); Allan P. Sindler, *Change in the Contemporary South* (Durham, N.C., 1963); William H. Nicholls, *Southern Tradition and Regional Progress* (Chapel Hill, N.C., 1960), and J. M. Maclachlan and J. S. Floyd, Jr., *This Changing South* (Gainesville, Fla., 1956).

Contemporary writers often reveal striking insight into their surroundings, and those who have observed and written about the Old South are no exception. Alexis de Tocqueville, *Democracy in America* (2 vols.; New York, 1841) is a French visitor's brilliant effort to interpret the American psychology, although he too simply traces the differences between northerners and southerners to slavery. An acute observer of the Southern scene was the New York landscape architect Frederick Law Olmsted, whose volumes were read with profit by men in both North and South: *A Journey in Seaboard Slave States* (New York, 1856), *A Journey in the Back Country* (New York, 1857), and *A Journey Through Texas* (New York, 1860). Hostile but brilliant were the observations of the English actress Frances A. Kemble in her *Journal of a Residence on a Georgia Plantation* (New York, 1863). Hinton Rowan Helper, *The Impending Crisis of the South* (New York, 1857) saw the South falling behind the North economically, attributing the deficiency to the deadening influence of slavery. A leading propagandist for

Southern views in the era of sectional conflict was George Fitzhugh. His *Sociology for the South, or the Failure of Free Society* (Richmond, 1854) and *Cannibals All: Or Slaves Without Masters* (Richmond, 1857) were attempts to defend the South and its institutions, particularly slavery, against the attacks of the abolitionists. Mary Boykin Chesnut in *A Diary from Dixie* (New York, 1905) records the keen observations of the wife of a South Carolina politician.

There has been no dearth of writers who have published their observations on the South since the Civil War. The contents of James S. Pike, *The Prostrate State: South Carolina under Negro Government* (New York, 1874) are revealed by the title. Charles H. Otken has written a competent statement on regional agricultural conditions in *The Ills of the South* (New York, 1894). Ray Stannard Baker, *Following the Color Line: An Account of Negro Citizenship in the American Democracy* (New York, 1908) is a Northern journalist's view that race relationships would and should be worked out gradually and quietly over a long course of years. Well written and filled with personal reflections of a passing way of life is William Alexander Percy, *Lanterns on the Levee: Recollections of a Planter's Son* (New York, 1941). *The Shore Dimly Seen* (Philadelphia, 1946) by Ellis G. Arnall contains the observations of a twentieth-century Georgia politician on conditions in the South. Arkansas Congressman Brooks Hays voices the silent thoughts of many southerners in his *A Southern Moderate Speaks* (Chapel Hill, N.C., 1959). The Atlanta *Constitution*'s Ralph McGill, a Pulitzer-prize winner in journalism, has written *The South and the Southerner* (Boston, 1964) which deals with the changing mores of the South. Mississippi newspaperman Hodding Carter has revealed his knowledge and understanding of his native region in a number of volumes, one of which deserves mention in this selected list: *Southern Legacy* (Baton Rouge, 1950). The story of the violent desegregation of the University of Mississippi is told by a personal witness to the events, faculty member James W. Silver. His volume, *Mississippi: The Closed Society* (New York, 1964), casts a long shadow across the entire South.

5